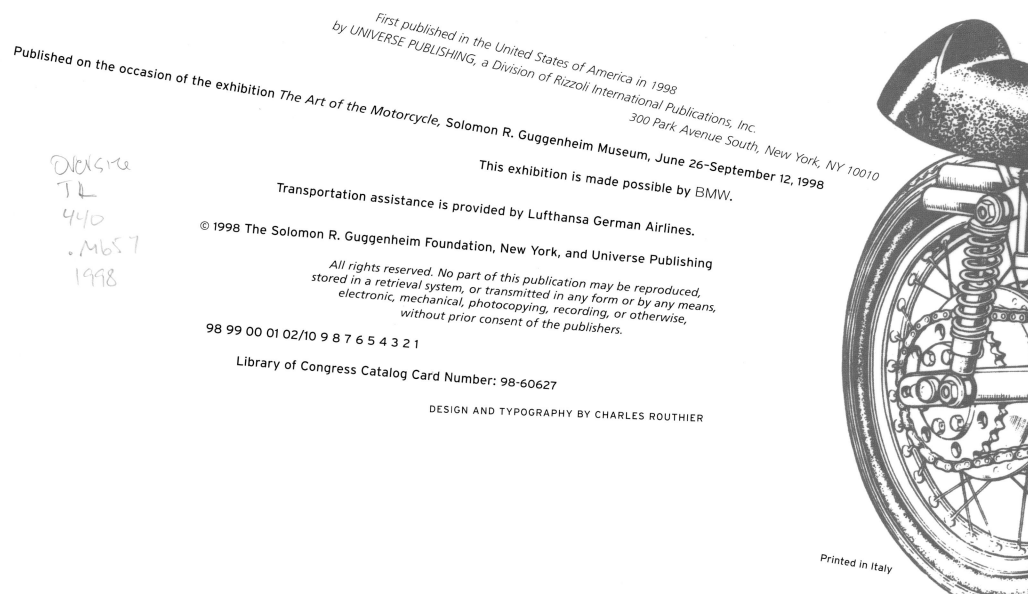

First published in the United States of America in 1998
by UNIVERSE PUBLISHING, a Division of Rizzoli International Publications, Inc.
300 Park Avenue South, New York, NY 10010

Published on the occasion of the exhibition The Art of the Motorcycle, Solomon R. Guggenheim Museum, June 26–September 12, 1998

This exhibition is made possible by BMW.

Transportation assistance is provided by Lufthansa German Airlines.

98 99 00 01 02/10 9 8 7 6 5 4 3 2 1

Library of Congress Catalog Card Number: 98-60627

DESIGN AND TYPOGRAPHY BY CHARLES ROUTHIER

Printed in Italy

Motorcycle Mania
The Biker Book

Guggenheim Museum

Edited by Matthew Drutt

Universe Publishing

Bike Culture

by Thomas Krens

The motorcycle and the art museum—these two cultural realms will intersect for the first time in the summer of 1998 in *The Art of the Motorcycle*, a landmark exhibition that brings together more than a century of bikes from around the world. Organized by the Solomon R. Guggenheim Museum, New York, the show opens with a historic collection of early experimental motorcycles, including the 1885 Daimler Einspur, and moves toward the future up to cutting-edge concept bikes that will define the machine in the twenty-first century. On proud display in the museum's famed Frank Lloyd Wright rotunda—one of the premier showcases for art of our century—these motorcycles have been selected both for their technical innovation and for their aesthetic merit.

There can be no doubt that the extraordinary motorcycles we have chosen belong in one of the world's great art museums; among the treasures on view are some the earliest motorcycles, such as the De Dion Bouton 247cc, made in France in 1899; the BMW R32, perhaps the most pioneering German motorcycle design; the Triumph Speed Twin, the 1938 British classic; the Honda 50 Super Cub from the 1950s, one of the most successful and widely sold motorcycles of all time; the 1977 Harley-Davidson XLCR, a radical styling departure for the oldest surviving American motorcycle manufacturer; and the Ducati 916, widely regarded as one of the most beautiful motorcycle designs ever produced.

The show also provides the opportunity to look at the enormous impact that a seemingly modest vehicle has had on our world. This book captures that spirit and the passion it has inspired in film, television, fashion, and popular culture. It complements the exhibition catalogue and uses the show as a springboard for a cultural celebration. Within its lively pages, readers will find a succinct design timeline based on the exhibition, featuring forty of the most significant motorcycles ever made. They are among the masterpieces that constitute *The Art of the Motorcycle*, but anyone who sees them knows that they transcend mere design excellence. Rather, they evoke desire and provoke the imagination—a world the editors of this book have aptly termed "motorcycle mania."

Motorcyclist astride his 1911-12 Yale, a marque popular in the United States between 1902 and 1915.

Motorcycle *Mania*

by Matthew Drutt

The first motorcycle was not intended as a revolution in two-wheeled transportation. Rather, Gottlieb Daimler and Wilhelm Maybach's 1885 *Reitwagen* was developed as a means to experiment with a gasoline engine for eventual incorporation into a four-wheeled motorized carriage. The inventors could hardly have imagined that their experiment would spawn one of the most powerful icons of modern culture. For the motorcycle has become more than just a vehicle: a hybrid of two great nineteenth-century achievements—the gasoline engine and the bicycle—the motorcycle is a reflection of our innate desire to change the shape of time and our relationship to the world around us through technological progress.

The motorcycle has come to signify a broad spectrum of values and ideas: from rebellion and the search for personal freedom to conformity, to control, to the quest for speed. Its impact can be felt in fashion, advertising, and popular culture. Time and again in film, television, music, and literature, the motorcycle has appeared as both demon and savior, a Janus-faced symbol of power and coming of age.

The earliest machines bear a distinct likeness to their ancestor, the bicycle. The Indian 500, Pierce Four, Flying Merkel, Cyclone, and others all retain the thin frame, seat, handlebar, and rotating pedal construction that we recognize in motorless cycles. By the 1920s, with the introduction of such machines as the English Scott Squirrel, something had clearly changed. The motorcycle had acquired the girth and solidity that distinguish it from pedal bikes, and new solutions to its design problems were sought. Engine performance also improved, so much that the motorcycle evolved into a machine capable of great speed. On April 14, 1920, Ernie Walker set the first world speed record for a motorcycle at Daytona on an Indian 994cc V-twin. He was clocked at 104 mph. (By contrast, today's machines can go three times that speed.)

One of the great superbike racers, Reg Pridmore is shown being followed into a fast corner during a race class.

The idea of racing motorcycles didn't take long to develop, and by 1904 the first major international event, the Coupe International, was held in France, with countries invited to enter up to three bikes each. By 1907, the celebrated Tourist Trophy event on the Isle of Man was born, considered for many years to be the most important international motorcycling event. That same year, the first concrete racetrack, Brooklands, was built in England, signaling the birth of today's controlled high-speed events. Other racing events started up in Italy, Spain, Germany, and the United States, testifying to the motorcycle's international status, and racing diversified into different classes and types, from track circuits to long-distance endurance competitions. The widespread popularity of racing, as strong today as ever, not only suggests bikers' fascination with speed and competition, but also their romantic inclination to impending danger.

> The great names in the motorcycle industry established themselves early on: Indian and Harley-Davidson in the United States; BMW, NSU, and DKW in Germany; BSA, Norton, and Triumph in Great Britain; Benelli and Moto Guzzi in Italy. But after World War II, such Japanese companies as Honda, Kawasaki, Suzuki, and Yamaha entered the picture and created new competition. Italy's Ducati—a company that would set new standards of elegance in design and identity—also emerged as an international force after the war.

Today's motorcycle is a far cry from its ancestors. A complex fusion of electronic engineering and computer design, it is a finely tuned machine built with lightweight materials and aerodynamic superiority. And yet, despite the transformations in technology, the basic bike is still being manufactured, and old bikes are salvaged, collected, restored, and revered. Thus, the motorcycle today exudes an aura of collective memory, summarizing the history of its past as it points toward the future. It is at once a crude and sophisticated object, built to go fast but also comfortable at leisurely speeds. It is as dangerous as it is safe; it is a badge of authority but also a symbol of rebellion.

> *Motorcycle Mania* is a journey through this diverse and complex landscape, mapping the history of the motorcycle's design and evolution and surveying the concurrent rise in cultural phenomena associated with it. The book both celebrates and deconstructs the popular stereotypes associated with bikers, exploring the rich paradoxes offered by a constituency made up of men and women, young and old, rich and poor, amateur and professional. In so doing, it confirms what people who ride bikes already know: the motorcycle is more than just a vehicle. It is a way of life.

(left) Racing toward the horizon during the 1993 Spanish Grand Prix. (right) Alberto Puig careens toward the finish line at the 500cc race of the 1995 Italian Grand Prix.

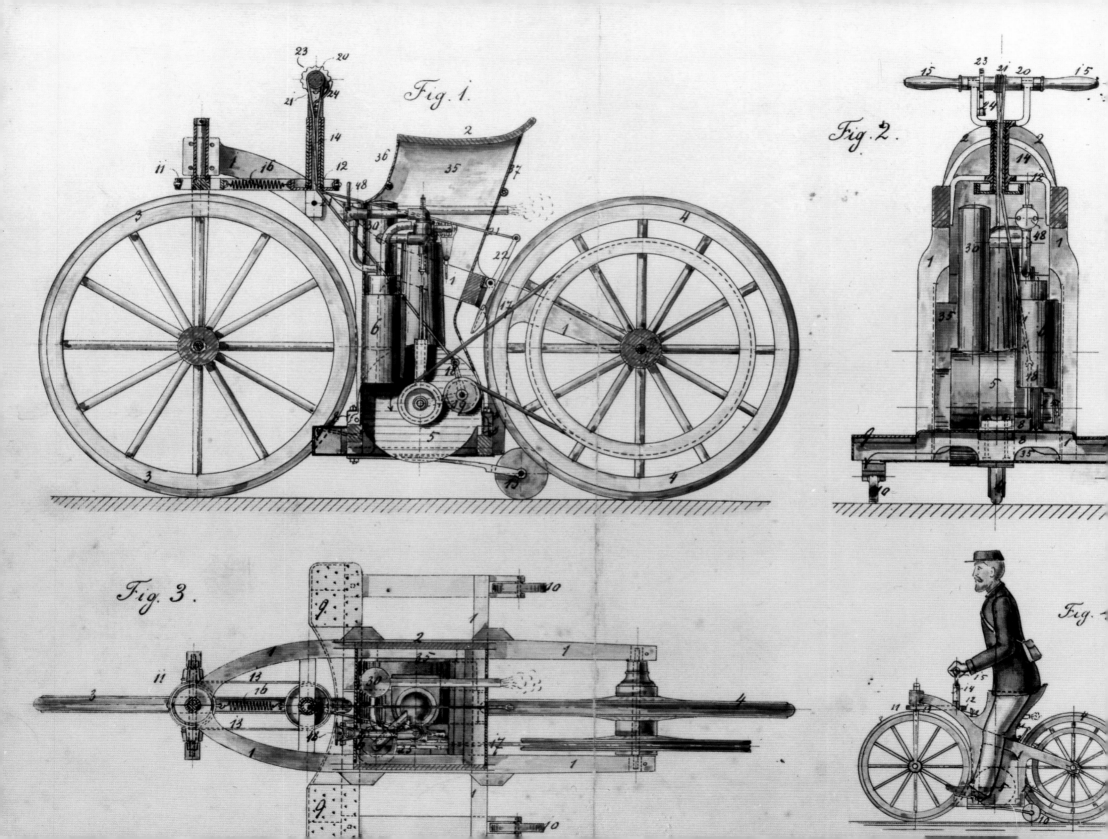

Fig. 1.

Fig. 2.

Fig. 3.

The *Machine*

by Wolfgang Dürheimer

Created in 1885 to test a new petroleum engine—almost as an accident, in fact—the motorcycle has changed little since. Clearly derived from the bicycle, the early motorcycles quickly found a standard: a pair of wheels, one behind the other, joined by a frame that placed the engine below and ahead of the rider, who, straddling the machine like a horse, perched atop a cacophonous assemblage of machinery. This format remains inherent in all motorcycles today. Since Daimler and Maybach's design, the engine remains in the middle of the motorcycle chassis, with a few unsuccessful attempts at modification, evidence that a powerful driving force can come from a simple, original source.

Worldwide, the majority of motorcycles use small, air-cooled, single-cylinder engines comparable to the Daimler *Reitwagen*; they are light, durable, and inexpensive to produce. However, in America the preference is clearly for multi-cylinder bikes, with the V-twin configuration, made viable by Harley-Davidson in the 1920s—a staple for many manufacturers. BMW's traditional opposed twin-cylinder configuration, called "boxer," continues to have a strong and loyal following. For larger motorcycles, the four-cylinder engine, with the cylinders arranged across the frame left to right, is the format of choice.

Overseas, the basic two-stroke engine—one that has no valves or camshafts and that produces twice as many power pulses as a four-stroke engine—has never been greatly improved. Small engines of this kind give young people their first push into motorized transportation. And because of its tremendous power-to-weight ratio, the two-stroke engine is dominant in worldwide motorcycle racing, producing as much as 200 horsepower from just 500cc. However, increasingly stringent emissions regulations have excluded the two-stroke from the American market; in 1985 the last street-legal two-stroke was sold here.

A single-cylinder Rotax-built engine, which powers BMW's F650 motorcycles, introduced in 1997.

The four-stroke engine, today usually made with four valves per cylinder, is dominant in the U.S. The number of cylinders in an engine is hardly an issue of price or status anymore, but rather a means of expressing personal taste. One- or two-cylinder bikes offer a robust display of power; three-, four-, or six-cylinder bikes have even more power and smoother capabilities. The possibilities of performance in bikes range from a mere 3 horsepower to a vigorous 150. At the high end, a multi-cylinder motorcycle has astonishing power: it can reach a speed of 60 miles per hour after only three seconds, well on the way to a top speed of 170 mph.

Though banished from modern automobiles, carburetors, which are simple and light, still supply many of today's motorcycles with fuel and air for the engine. Fuel-injection systems, such as the ones BMW has mass-produced for the last decade, are quickly catching up as the U.S. Environmental Protection Agency tightens its grip on emissions from all sources. BMW, Harley-Davidson, and many others are jumping on the fuel-injection bandwagon because the bikes run better and are more efficient with fuel injection.

In spite of developments, motorcycle technology clings to the virtues of simplicity, in great measure because weight plays a large role in a bike's performance. Add 100 pounds to a sedan and the performance will not change; add the same 100 pounds to a 500-pound motorcycle and performance falls dramatically. Until the 1970s, bikes' electrical systems were elementary, commonly without electric starting, a feature we take for granted in automobiles. With small bikes and off-road bikes, the kick-starter, formerly the common method of starting every bike, is only now fading. However, the headlights of motorcycles draw upon the same modern technology as the automobile—even the lowliest of economy models has a bright headlight with a halogen bulb. Many new models boast projector-style beams or multi-faceted reflectors.

Drive from the engine to the rear wheel—there are no front-wheel-drive motorcycles—is accomplished most often with a chain. Though noisy and dirty, a chain is still the lightest and most efficient way to transfer power from the engine to the ground. There are a few exceptions, however. Harley-Davidson employs a belt drive instead of a chain, and as early as 1923 BMW had transplanted an automobile's final-drive gears onto the motorcycle, resulting in what is called shaft drive. All but one of BMW's current models uses shaft drive, and many touring bikes use this method because it is durable, quiet, and clean; at the same time, it is understood to consume too much power and to be too heavy for high-performance applications.

On BMW's 1998 R1200C motorcycle, the drive shaft housing does double duty as the bike's single-sided swing arm, which mates the rear wheel to the chassis.

Anatomy of a Motorcycle

Not much has changed in motorcycle construction. The elements remain basically the same, although new technologies (ABS, alloy metals, carbon fiber, fuel injection) have thoroughly modernized each component: an exposed chassis and engine (sometimes forming part of the chassis), hand- and foot-operated brakes (hydraulic and cable), clutch (engaged via the left hand), transmission (most often operated with the left foot), two wheels (or three with a sidecar or trikes), and suspension. Using this vintage diagram, we begin to see the simplicity of this seemingly complex machine.

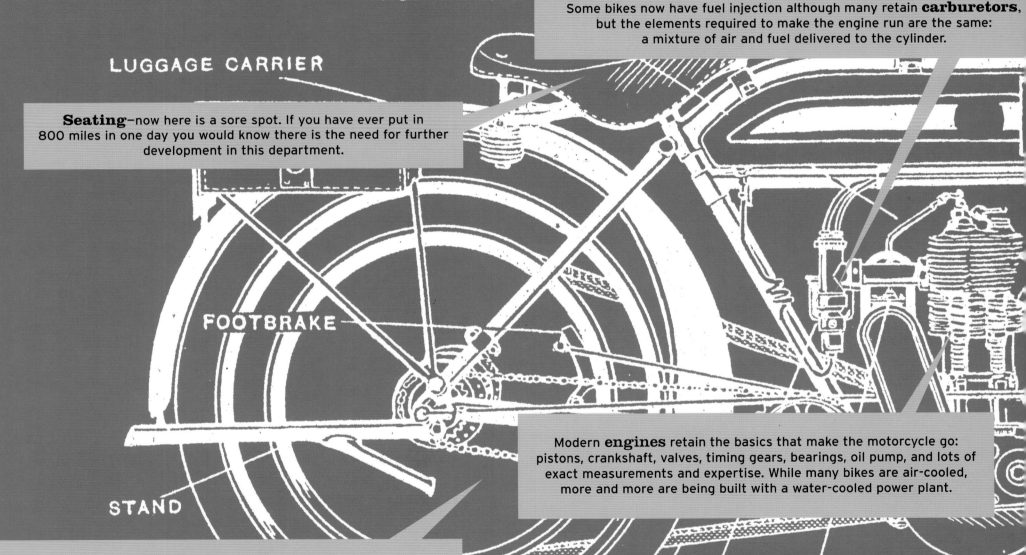

HIGH TENSION

LUGGAGE CARRIER

Some bikes now have fuel injection although many retain **carburetors**, but the elements required to make the engine run are the same: a mixture of air and fuel delivered to the cylinder.

Seating—now here is a sore spot. If you have ever put in 800 miles in one day you would know there is the need for further development in this department.

FOOTBRAKE

STAND

Modern **engines** retain the basics that make the motorcycle go: pistons, crankshaft, valves, timing gears, bearings, oil pump, and lots of exact measurements and expertise. While many bikes are air-cooled, more and more are being built with a water-cooled power plant.

Connecting the transmission to the rear wheel, most bikes use either a **chain**, **drive shaft**, or **belt**. Motorcycle transmissions use five or six forward gears to keep the engine within its powerband.

MAGNETO

CARBURETTER

BELT

The **handlebars** contain controls to keep both hands busy. The throttle is a twist grip in the right hand and the clutch is operated by a lever attached to the left side of the handlebar. Highbeams and turn signals are managed by switches just inboard of the handgrips. Mounted in the center of the handlebars are the tachometer, speedometer, and miscellaneous warning lights.

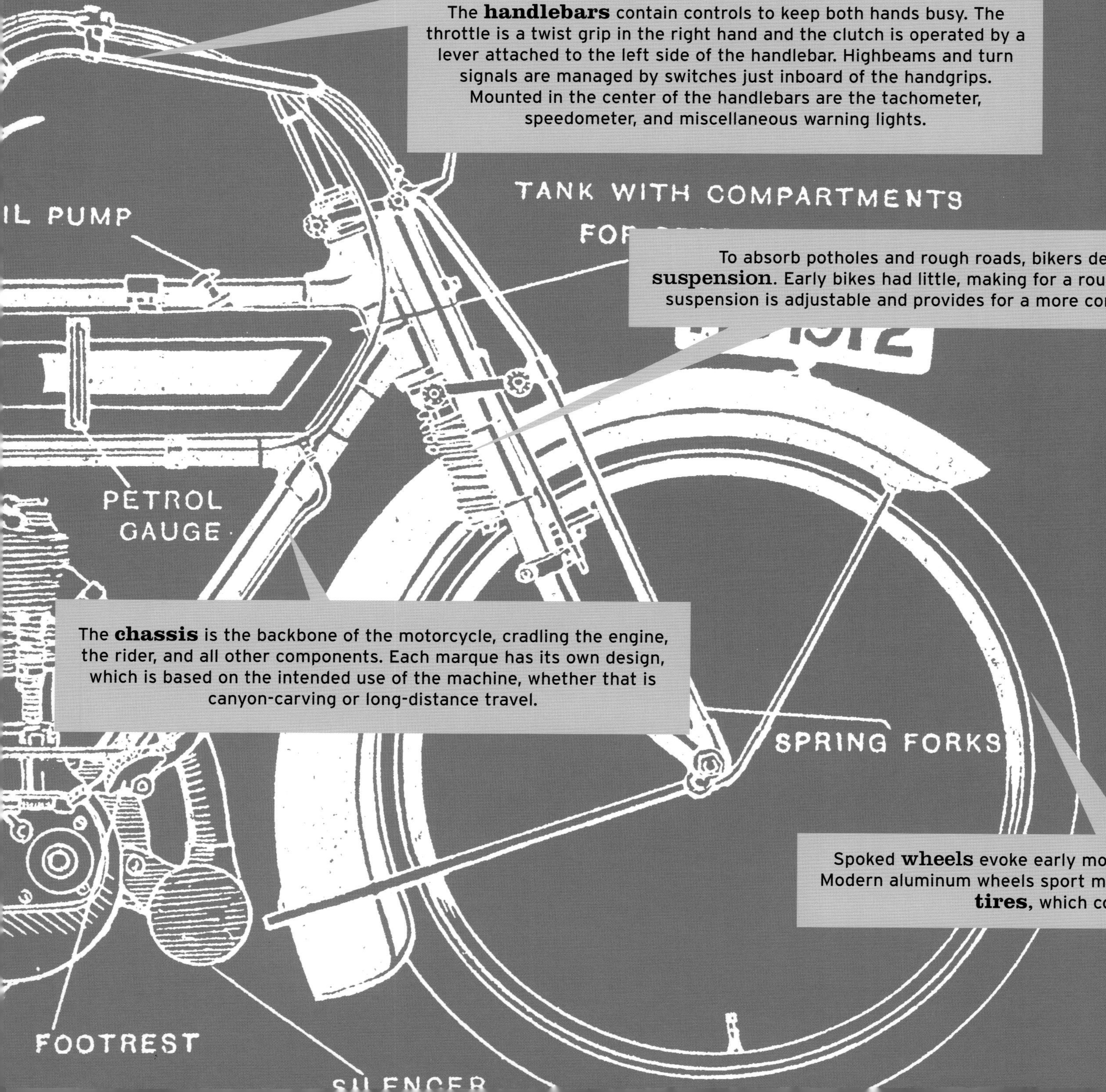

TANK WITH COMPARTMENTS
FOR

IL PUMP

To absorb potholes and rough roads, bikers depend on **suspension**. Early bikes had little, making for a rough ride, but now suspension is adjustable and provides for a more comfortable ride.

PETROL
GAUGE

The **chassis** is the backbone of the motorcycle, cradling the engine, the rider, and all other components. Each marque has its own design, which is based on the intended use of the machine, whether that is canyon-carving or long-distance travel.

SPRING FORKS

Spoked **wheels** evoke early models but need to be periodically adjusted. Modern aluminum wheels sport more futuristic designs and can use tubeless **tires**, which come in all different sizes.

FOOTREST

SILENCER

Automatic transmissions, now the most popular choice in cars, can be found only in scooters. True motorcycles have five or six manual synchronized gears, and a few large touring bikes even have reverse. Convention now dictates that the clutch is activated with the left hand, while the gears are changed with a small lever by the left foot. Early motorcycles succumbed to the whims of their designers, some with right-foot shifting, others with hand shifters near the fuel tank. Motorcycle transmissions are sequential—shifting must take place in order; in other words, first, then second, then third.

Motorcycle chassis design has been thoroughly transformed since Daimler and Maybach's wooden prototype. The completely suspensionless "boneshaker" gained rudimentary suspension by the beginning of this century. The first spring outfitting of the rear-wheel suspension was introduced in the 1930s, although many bikes from the 1910s employed front forks with a small amount of suspension travel. Even so, the rider's best friend in those times was a generously sprung saddle. The latest state-of-the-art engineering for front wheels is the highly evolved telescopic fork, which has many adjustments and has gained tremendously in size and stiffness in the last decade. BMW's Telelever front suspension borrows from automotive design, offering more suppleness than a conventional fork, with the other benefits of an A-arm design.

Refined shocks and carefully chosen springs are the general standard. Street machines now spoil their riders and side-car passengers with long-travel suspension, allowing about six inches of wheel movement to absorb bumps. Professional off-road bikes provide for almost twice that amount to bounce over rough ground. With most bikes, the suspension is capable of myriad adjustments, fine-tuning the bike to the rider's weight and preferred riding style.

Wheels frequently determine the character of a motorcycle. Off-road bikes and cruisers still roll in elegance on wire-spoke wheels, the traditional style, dating back more than 100 years. Cast wheels made of light metal are now the fashion for conventional street bikes and wilder superbikes; lightness, durability, and the ability to use tubeless tires are their main selling points. Harley-Davidson's Fat Boy offered a new alternative in 1990 with entirely smooth wheels, front and rear, made of cast aluminum. Even though the 16-inch cast wheels were heavier than spokes, the look made the Fat Boy an instant success.

Since the introduction of the disc brake at the end of the 1960s, motorcycle brakes have become stronger and more agile in direct response to greater grip from new tires and from the fabulous power available even to midsize machines. The front wheel brake, often with two discs, is operated by the right hand, while the back wheel brake reacts to downward pressure on the right foot pedal. There is no power assistance; good motorcycle brakes can be activated with two fingers or even one toe until they lock. Combination brakes, in which one hand or foot activates both front and rear brakes, as in automobiles, are an exception with motorcycles because a good rider can adjust the brake-force distribution to different street surfaces better than any hydraulic system. However, motorcycles with antilock systems are quickly becoming more popular: BMW produces a large percentage of bikes with ABS.

Tire design has seen the greatest advances. The most prominent feature now is size: the width of the rear wheel has doubled in the last twenty years. Common now are rear tires 190 mm wide—a figure approaching that of many automobiles. Moreover, specialization is boundless: motorcycles have rear tires in different dimensions with differing profiles and rubber compounds, the principal purpose being to develop grip according to bike size.

But tire producers cannot change the fact that 80 percent of the bike's braking power is transmitted to the ground by a patch of rubber the size of a man's fist, or that accelerative performance of more than 100 horsepower flows onto the road over a rear-wheel contact patch no larger than a shoe sole. For many riders—sporting types in particular—durability is a secondary issue to absolute grip, reliability, and good handling qualities. (A rear tire of a superbike can wear out after 1,000 or after 5,000 miles, depending on the temper of its rider.) Many bike manufacturers test dozens of different compounds and profiles before releasing a production specification, all in search of that elusive ideal balance between performance and durability.

Modern technology plays a major role in the complexity of today's bikes. Early bike manufacturers didn't have the benefit of testing their machines in a wind tunnel, which allows the controlled study of wind resistance and has resulted in sleeker designs. Fully faired bikes didn't benefit from wind-tunnel research until the BMW R100RS was introduced in the 1970s. On motorcycles with perfect aerodynamics it is now possible for rider and sidecar passenger to travel through rain and remain nearly dry. But for many hardcore bikers, this is too much progress.

Repair and Rapport

One of the great joys of owning a motorcycle is the ability to repair it. While more sophisticated machines may not lend themselves to easy fixing, the basic bike can be pulled apart and reassembled by the average person. Replacing worn parts and tuning the engine creates an intimate bond between owner and machine that some have construed as transcendent, like Robert Pirsig in *Zen and the Art of Motorcycle Maintenance*:

> Each machine has its own, unique personality which probably could be defined as the intuitive sum total of everything you know and feel about it. This personality constantly changes, usually for the worse, but sometimes surprisingly for the better, and it is this personality that is the real object of motorcycle maintenance.

(left) Getting ready to restore a 1930s Harley-Davidson.

Riding Tips

It's almost as easy as riding a bike, though riding a motorcycle requires quite a bit more agility and coordination, not to mention self-confidence. Still, the modern-day machine is so finely crafted and designed that getting it going rarely requires the elbow grease that older machines demanded. However, early machines were not exactly the pinnacle of comfort; thus many handbooks for riding included now such time-honored tips as the following:

Comfort in Motorcycling There are many who firmly believe that the motorcycle is uncomfortable. But I can assure them that it need not be so, and I will go so far as to say that unless the rider is perfectly comfortable, and unless he feels as at home on his machine as in his own armchair, he cannot obtain the best results. J. HARRISON, FROM *HOW TO RIDE A MOTOR CYCLE: A HANDBOOK FOR BOTH NOVICES AND EXPERIENCED MOTOR CYCLISTS*, 1927.

Some Hints to Lady Passengers Never travel with a driver in whom you have not complete confidence, and avoid any machine that is not equipped with a proper seat and foot-rests. I always ride astride as it is far safer and more comfortable. Sit quite naturally—as in a chair—and do not attempt to steer the machine by moving your body; the driver will do all that is necessary in this respect . . . . Sit as near to him as possible in order to distribute the weight evenly over the two wheels. PHOEBE HARRISON, IN *HOW TO RIDE A MOTOR CYCLE: A HANDBOOK FOR BOTH NOVICES AND EXPERIENCED MOTOR CYCLISTS*, 1927.

(right) A good riding position for comfort: the rider's weight should be properly divided between the saddle, foot-rests, and handlebars. FROM *THE MOTOR CYCLE BOOK FOR BOYS*, 1928

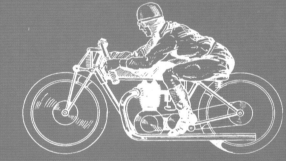

FIG. 96 UNCOMFORTABLE RIDING POSITION. SUITABLE FOR RACING ONLY

FIG. 97 NATURAL ATTITUDE, SUITABLE FOR TOURING AND FAST ROAD WORK

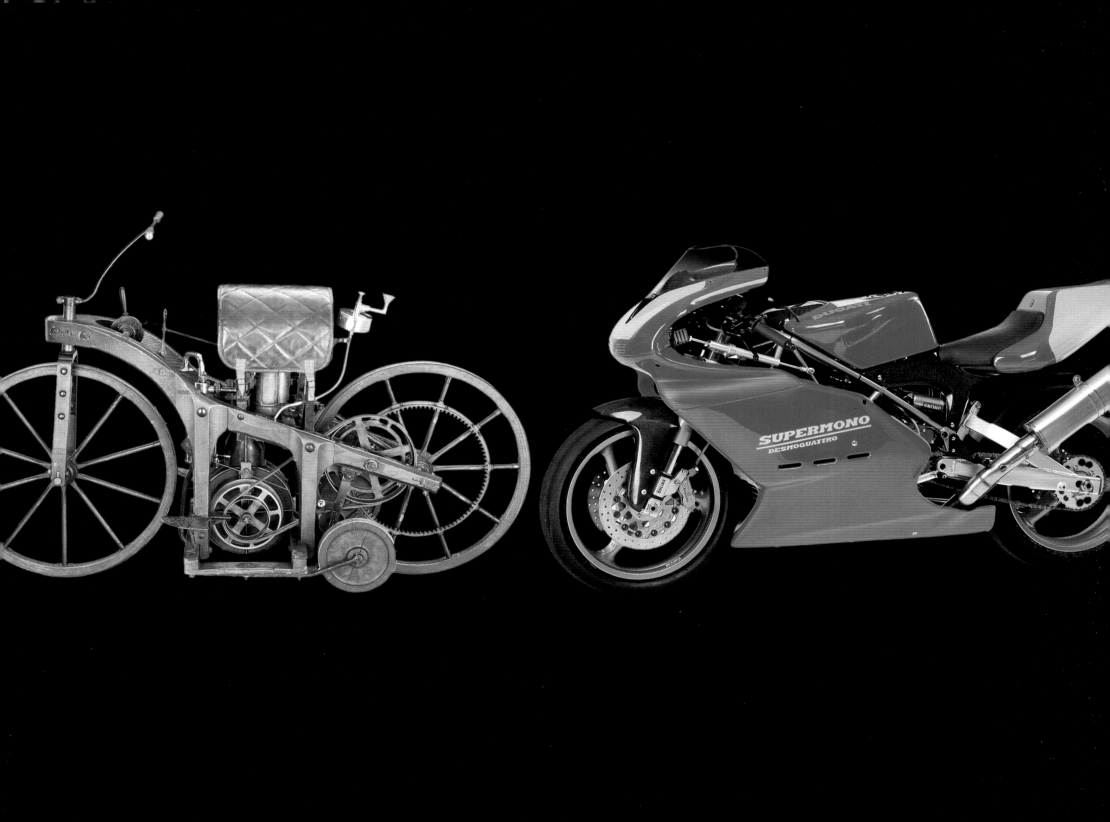

Dressed Up, Stripped Down

by Jon Thompson

In the beginning, there was the motorcycle, and it was completely without style. The year was 1885. Daimler, the venerable inventor of the automobile, cobbled up a two-wheeled test platform for his internal-combustion engine, wheeled his contraption from his workshop in Cannstatt, Germany, fired it up, and doubtless frightened the bejesus out of the townsfolk.

Though it featured the basic elements of the machines that would follow it—two wheels, an engine, and a chassis—Daimler's machine was an entirely accidental invention of something for which there was neither need nor market. By the late 1890s, however, as people responded to the wonderful and frightening assortment of possibilities offered by the rapidly changing technology of the dawning century, including the gas-powered internal-combustion engine, motorized two-wheel transport was in production in Europe and the United States. And by 1901, when Hendee Manufacturing began building Indians in Massachusetts, motorcycle companies were thriving in northern Europe and the United States.

Like Daimler's *Reitwagen*, these machines were champions of function over form: the need to efficiently package engine, fuel supply, and rider overwhelmed any desire to make the things stylish. To be sure, there were stylistic differences between an Indian, say, and a Harley-Davidson, whose first machines were produced in 1903. But these were differences of detail in the engineering approach to a common problem: the way the sheet metal of a fuel tank or a fender was formed, for example.

Daimler's *Reitwagen* (1885), the first motorcycle prototype, faces Ducati's Supermono (1993), exemplifying today's elegant and sporty designs.

With their pioneering spirit and desire to be different, Americans had difficulty leaving their motorcycles alone. If they could add special pieces to dress up their machines, they did, in part because those early machines were incredibly elemental. They needed innovation and improvement. But as bikes became more complete through the 1930s, this urge to customize began to demand a stripped-down approach, especially in California, where moderate weather minimized the need for protection afforded by fenders and bodywork. Riders began bobbing fenders, chopping frames, extending forks, and swapping and modifying gas tanks. Style was becoming as important as function. Following World War II, customizing became even more exaggerated when a few restless folk began building choppers, perhaps the ultimate in stretched-out, stripped-down rides. The motorcycle became a rolling example of personal expression.

But this was styling by popular decree, accomplished post-factory. Style-by-factory came from the pencil of a young British visionary named Edward Turner, who possessed an impossible personality and an uncanny feel for line and proportion. With the German armies lapping at the shores of the British Isles, Turner, influenced by the machine aesthetics of the Continent's Bauhaus and Art Nouveau movements, created the Triumph Speed Twin in 1939, an elegantly simple design that just looked and felt right. It may be one of the motor industry's longest-lasting concepts, for the Speed Twin's design elements—the classically tapered fuel tank and the sweep of its twin exhaust pipes—continued in production after World War II and as staples of the Triumph line through the end of Triumph production in the early 1970s. Indeed, the all-new line of Triumph motorcycles, revived in 1990 by businessman John Bloor, now sports two models that borrow developments of Turner's original tank shape and exhaust sweep.

At the same time Turner was setting the tone for elegant simplicity, the Indian Motocycle Company, of Springfield, Massachusetts, was preparing a machine that would have almost as much an impact on motorcycle style as the Triumph. Mechanically, this new Indian, the 1940 Chief, was much like the previous models. But it wore outrageous sheet metal in the form of fenders that enclosed nearly half of each wheel with skirt-like valences. These two machines, the '39 Triumph and the '40 Indian, set the tone for what was to come. The Triumph, a model of elegant simplicity, represented the stripped-down look, and the Indian, in its glamorous excess, stood for the dressed-up look.

(clockwise from top left) **1996 Triumph Adventurer** Though it is separated from the Speed Twin's design by nearly 60 years, Triumph in the 1990s returned to the "classic" look (note the shape of its fuel tank, which mimics that of the 1939 bike).

1998 Triumph T508 If the Adventurer proves that history can offer design inspiration, this machine illustrates that the same company can point to the future with inspired design.

1947 Indian Chief Nearly identical to the 1940 version, which debuted these sweeping fender valences. If the 1939 Triumph is stripped down, this bike is definitely dressed up.

1939 Triumph Speed Twin A 500cc masterpiece from the easel of Edward Turner, and a bike whose basic lines, especially the profile of the fuel tank, are reflected today in the lines of some modern Triumph models.

Grand prix racers in the 350cc class exit a corner during the 1956 running of the Grand Prix of Germany. These bikes wear what are called dustbin fairings, most often formed from thin sheets of aluminum.

Fairings like this, enclosing a machine's front wheel, were eventually banned, ostensibly because of fears of crosswind-induced instability.

The science of aerodynamics and the post-war rebirth of international motorcycle roadracing also exerted more than a little influence. European roadracing bikes began to show up in the early 1950s with fully enclosed and streamlined bodywork called fairings. Form thus became function, in that fairings were seen to contribute to a machine's aerodynamic slipperiness and therefore to its top speed. Early examples were clumsy-looking and ill-received. Nonbelievers referred to them as "dustbins," British vernacular for trash cans. Dustbin fairings, which enclosed even the front wheel, eventually were expelled from organized racing because riders feared they were vulnerable to instability in crosswinds, but these early fairings pointed the way to the now almost ubiquitous fiberglass fairing work on sportbikes found in Ducati, Suzuki, Kawasaki, Honda, and Yamaha showrooms.

Honda, certainly the most powerful of the Japanese manufacturers, created a new standard with its Gold Wing touring bike, which wore an all-enclosing fairing. Streamlining wasn't the point. Stylish weather protection was. Touring bikes had worn various forms of weather protection, but none of these was as complete or as attractive as the all-enclosing plastic that draped the big Honda. These were the ultimate in dressed-up motorcycles, coming fully equipped with everything a rider could want. Yet the Japanese bike manufacturers were ever-versatile: the plastic-faired 1986 Suzuki GSX-R7650, seen by some observers as the first modern sportbike, embodied the essence of the stripped-down look.

Honda's Gold Wing touring bike. This top-of-the-line SE version includes virtually all the options of an automobile except air-conditioning and is among the ultimate in dressed-up rides. Enclosing everything in plastic eliminates the need to apply fine finishes to weld, frame, and engine surfaces hidden under the fairing.

If art, science, and racing competition have played roles in the evolution of motorcycle style, so has economics. As mass production and technology allowed for better and more reliable equipment, enthusiasts could afford to buy motorcycles as much for how they looked as for how they worked. Now, in a reversal of roles, form has become at least as important as function, and in some cases, maybe more so.

Don't believe it? Check the enormous prices on the pieces of rolling art created by such stylists as Louie Netz and Willie G. Davidson at Harley-Davidson. Custom artists like Arlen Ness and Bob Dron, of the San Francisco Bay area, specialize in Harley styling, and both have been hugely influential, with their designs spawning legions of custom motorcycles. This liberation on the street has led to factory-created gorgeous faired and unfaired Ducatis designed by Massimo Tamburini and Michelangel Galluzzi, the avant-look BMWs drawn by David Robb (like Galluzzi, a graduate of the Art Center College of Design in Pasadena, California), the industrial-think Aprilias from the drafting board of Philippe Starck, and the amazing variety of equipment being produced by unheralded, indeed often corporately anonymous, artists and designers at the Japanese bike companies.

Free-thinking is, after all, what began it all: the freedom to rely on the use of a spinning wheel's gyroscopic stability and thus travel on two wheels instead of four, the freedom to transport oneself economically, the freedom to buy or build a motorcycle pretty much in any shape or form that can be imagined.

And don't forget the most important freedom of all—the rhapsodic freedom a rider experiences when he climbs on his dressed-up or stripped-down motorcycle—it doesn't matter which—and heads out with the wind in his face and the knowledge in his heart and mind that whatever form his ride takes, it's something special, something that reflects exactly his ideas about what a proper motorcycle should look and feel like.

The 1998 Ducati Monster.
The brainchild of Cagiva designer Michelangel Galluzzi,
the 900cc Monster is one of the best examples of the stripped-down hotrod.

The K1200RS BMW (1998). Once upon a time motorcycle chassis were very simple assemblies of mild-steel tubing. Today they're pieces of practical art. Note that this BMW's backbone frame is composed of welded aluminum castings, and that the fairing from the same bike (above right) is very carefully modeled to cleave the air and protect the rider from inclement weather.

Merely Motorcycles or Something More?

It is perhaps too easy to dismiss the motorcycle. Sure, for a few, they are essential, everyday vehicles. For most, however, they're luxury items, toys, technological fluff. And yet some of the most creative motor-vehicle designers ever to pick up pencil and protractor are drawn to them, moths to the hot flame of creative possibility.

Ron Hill, chairman of the transportation design department, Art Center College of Design, Pasadena, California, says, "Whether it's a composer or a motorcycle designer, someone has to think about the future. It's difficult to do. Doing so is subjective, intuitive, and emotional. It's not quantifiable." And yet design quantifies. It overlays technology with identity and character and soul. All are qualities without shape or form, but like a camper meeting his first grizzly bear, we know them when we see them. BMW, Ducati, Harley-Davidson, and Honda all understand this very well. All have attracted specialists to help them establish their design identities.

For Martin Manchester, a designer at American Honda, the job is elegant and simple. It is, he says, "using proportions to express a concept." But for David Robb, motorcycle design director at BMW, things are a little more complicated: "These products have got to reflect society, and the kind of moods we're in. I ask myself, what's the soul of this thing? What do people want to do with this object? How do we communicate that?" So if Robb is right, part of the design ideal involves tapping into the social psyche; part of it involves using what's gone before to explore what's coming; part of it involves the sometimes opposing concepts of form and function.

At Harley-Davidson, form and function aren't separated. They're united in a cordial synthesis that adds a surprising and elusive third ingredient. As explained by designer Louie Netz, "Our design chief, Willie G. Davidson says, and this is so accurate, in motorcycle design form follows function. But they both report to emotion." Ah, emotion. The way motorcycles make us feel. Is that what it's about?

For Massimo Tamburini, the celebrated chief of the Cagiva Research Center in the principality of San Marino, and the man responsible not just for the aesthetics of the Ducati 916, but also for the chassis that allows it to be such an incredibly effective sporting tool, there's a practical aspect few of the product's end users would ever consider. Tamburini says, "I think about the shape as possessed by everyone who will share it. I'm not only talking about the rider, but also about the worker who will have to assemble the bike, and the mechanic who will have to service it. Each time a new bike goes out from the Cagiva Research Center, we all ask ourselves, 'Is that the best we can do?'"

Still, in the end, this concept of design remains as elusive and fragile as a wisp of high-octane exhaust smoke. The Art Center's Hill explains that, at its root form, "design comes from the creative urge to make a statement. This creativity can't be taught. It's innate. We just have to be sure we don't allow society to beat it out of us."

JON THOMPSON

The *Design Evolution* of the

by **Matthew Drutt** and **Vanessa Rocco**, with assistance from Kevin Cameron, Clement Salvadore, Brian Slark, and Daniel Statnekov

Choosing which bikes are pivotal in the history of the motorcycle's evolution is a topic as hotly debated as which sports team is best. A hundred different people would likely have a hundred different lists. The following selection has been made to show fundamental shifts in the design, architecture, and technology of the motorcycle. It is offered as a guide, and includes some of the more idiosyncratic designs in the history of motorcycles.

Indian Single 260cc, 1901 (USA)
Collection Otis Chandler Vintage Museum of Transportation and Wildlife

This bike is one of only two Indian "motocycles" built in 1901, the year the company was founded. The single-cylinder engine bikes produced between 1901 and 1908 retained a bicycle-style diamond frame.

Machine

The Flying Merkel Model "V" 884cc, 1911 (USA)
*Collection Otis Chandler Vintage Museum
of Transportation and Wildlife*

This motorcycle is a map of such early mechanical features as belt transmissions, yet it also incorporates Joseph Merkel's innovations, including the throttle-controlled lubrication system.

**Cyclone Stripped Stock Model 7R-14
1000cc, 1914 (USA)**
Collection Daniel K. Statnekov

Produced 1912-17, the Cyclone was initially the only commercial producer of 996cc V-twins with an overhead camshaft. It won many races until bigger factories such as Harley came out with an 8-valve V-twin.

Pierce Four 696cc, 1910 (USA)
Collection Otis Chandler Vintage Museum of Transportation and Wildlife

In 1909, the Pierce Cycle Company of Buffalo, New York, introduced the first four-cylinder motorcycle to be manufactured in the United States. From its inception, the Pierce Four was intended to achieve the same standard of excellence as the Pierce-Arrow automobile. Inspired by the successful design of the four-cylinder "FN" manufactured in Belgium by Fabrique Nationale d'Arms de Guerre, Pierce company engineers built their own version of an in-line four-cylinder motor and along with it designed a state-of-the-art motorcycle.

Iver-Johnson Model 15-7 1016cc, 1915 (USA)

Collection Otis Chandler Vintage Museum of Transportation and Wildlife

Iver became known as the aristocrat among motorcycles. The fluid arch of the frame above the engine, the sculpted fuel tanks, and the austere paint scheme all contributed to this reputation.

Harley-Davidson W Sport Twin 584cc, 1919 (USA)

Collection Otis Chandler Vintage Museum of Transportation and Wildlife

The Twin was designed to attract a more general public than Harley had been targeting. It was light and easily controllable, with a small number of oil compartments that guaranteed a cleaner ride, further contributing to its mass appeal.

Indian 8-valve Board Track Racer 1000cc, 1915 (USA)

Collection Daniel K. Statnekov

The 8-valve was designed to regain Indian's dominance on the racetrack, and the increased number (from four) and overhead design of the valves proved unbeatable. This machine was never offered to the public, and the few produced were ridden by professionals.

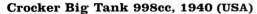

Crocker Big Tank 998cc, 1940 (USA)
*Collection Otis Chandler Vintage Museum of
Transportation and Wildlife*

The Crocker was completely handcrafted, serving as a forerunner to post-war customization. The dramatically designed fuel tank and the rich color scheme of the chassis perfectly suit this powerful five-hundred-pound machine.

Gnome et Rhone M1 306cc, 1934 (France)
Collection The Barber Vintage Motorsports Museum

Established in 1919, Gnome et Rhone was an innovative company famous for their World War I aircraft engines. This bike demonstrates the continental flair for design, particularly in its perimeter frame.

Sunbeam S7 487cc, 1947 (UK)
Collection The Barber Vintage Motorsports Museum

The post-war Sunbeam set new standards in style and comfort; the power unit is mounted in rubber, isolating engine vibration. There are only thirteen known 1947 models in existence.

Scott Squirrel Sprint Special
620cc 1929 (UK)
Collection The Barber Vintage Motorsports Museum

Alfred Angus Scott was a pioneer in the industry. He began producing two-stroke motorcycles in 1908, which included revolutionary features such as the triangulated frame, water-cooled engines, and fuel injection. He went on to hold sixty separate motorcycle patents. This example was built to compete in vintage racing competitions, such as the Isle of Man TT, and was so superior in performance to competitors (which were little more than souped-up bicycles) that it was frequently banned from events.

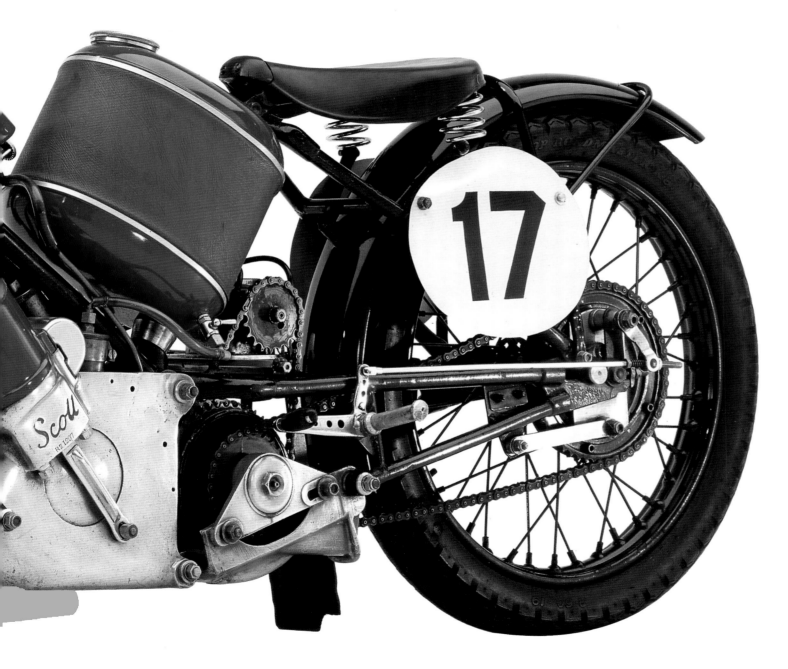

JAP Speedway Bike 500cc, 1949 (UK)
Collection The Barber Vintage Motorsports Museum

In 1928, John A. Prestwick became interested in speedway racing, a form of racing in which the bikes have no brakes. He set out to develop the now-famous JAP Speedway engines, which remain virtually unchanged and still compete successfully.

AJS E95 500 Road Racer 499cc, 1953 (UK)
Collection The Barber Vintage Motorsports Museum

This bike is a redesigned version of the "Porcupine," whose nickname was derived from its unusual, spiky cylinder head. The original design for this model was meant for supercharged engines, which became 'illegal' after World War II, as they had an unfair advantage in races.

Gilera Saturno 499cc, 1947 (Italy)
Collection Otis Chandler Vintage Museum of Transportation and Wildlife

The Saturno quickly became the most popular model Giuseppe Gilera produced, due to its clean lines, excellent road performance, and successful racing results.

Harley-Davidson Sportster XL 883cc, 1957 (USA)
*Collection Otis Chandler Vintage Museum
of Transportation and Wildlife*

Harley was just beginning to woo customers away from British makes when the Sportster debuted. Due to improved engine performance and cosmetic enhancements, sales climbed.

MV Agusta 500 Grand Prix 499cc, 1956 (Italy)
Collection The Barber Vintage Motorsports Museum

This GP is one of the machines that gave Sir John Surtees and MV Agusta their first 500cc World Championship in 1956. MV Agusta continued to rule the world championship circuits into the 60s and 70s.

Vincent Black Shadow Series C 998cc 1954 (UK)
*Collection Otis Chandler Vintage Museum
of Transportation and Wildlife*

The Series C was in production from 1949 until 1954, a time when it was considered the fastest motorcycle in the world. This bike was one of the last of this series built.

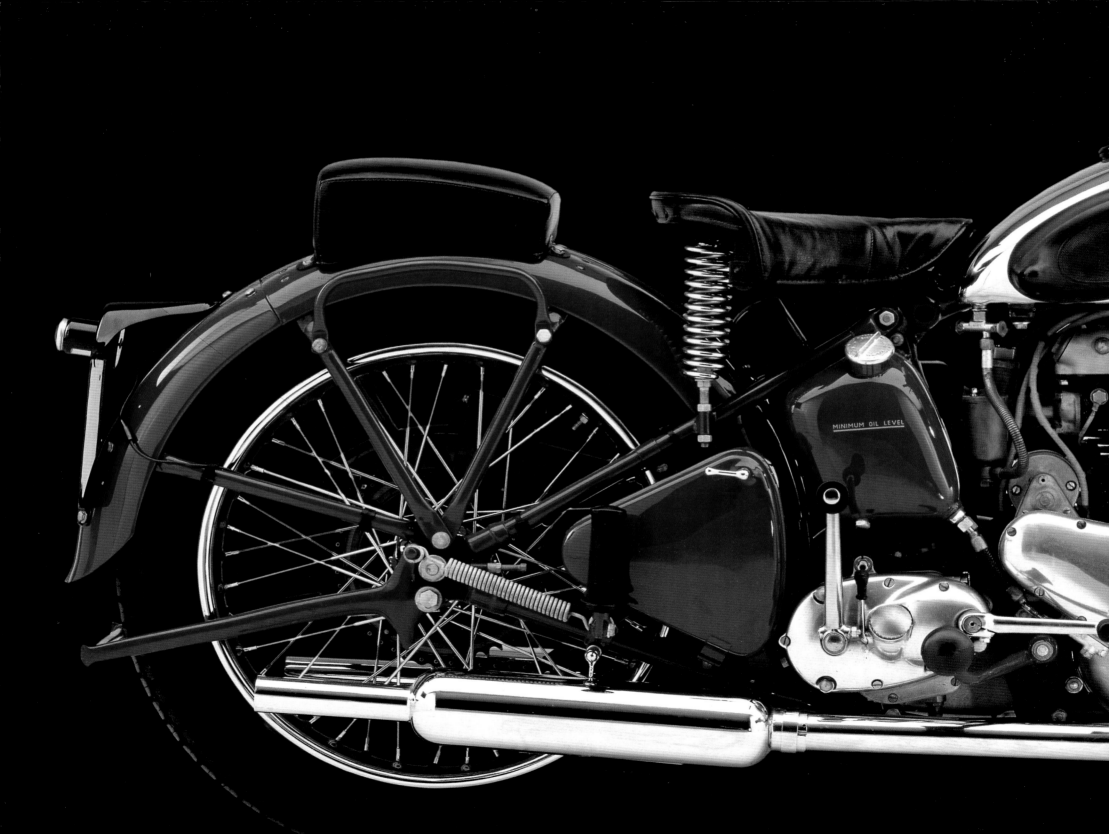

Triumph Speed Twin 498cc 1938 (UK)
Collection The Barber Vintage Motorsports Museum

The Speed Twin is the definitive first example of the parallel-twin design that would dominate post-war British motorcycle production, with BSA, Matchless, AJS, and Norton all producing bikes with similar engines. Veteran engineer Doug Hele has said that this engine type was the only one post-war Britain could afford to produce in quantity. Triumph entered the motorcycle business in 1903, building singles for many years. The Speed Twin represents a cost-effective compromise between the market's desire for something smoother and more powerful than a single, yet less complex and expensive than multi-cylinder engines.

Honda CR 110 50cc, 1962 (Japan)
Collection The Barber Vintage Motorsports Museum

This model was a production roadracer, but Honda also made a street version. It was very unusual at the time to find a 50cc bike with a four-stroke engine, and the construction allowed for tremendous rpm.

Triumph Twenty-One 350cc, 1958 (UK)
Collection The Barber Vintage Motorsports Museum

Designer Edward Turner's heavy bodywork styling on the Twenty-One was more popular in Europe than in America where the market felt it wasn't "macho" unless all the machinery was exposed.

Harley-Davidson KR 750cc, 1957 (USA)
Collection The Barber Vintage Motorsports Museum

KRs were the racing Harleys in the 1950s and 60s. This bike was ridden by Roger Reiman in the first Daytona to be run on a speedway instead of on the beach.

BSA Gold Star Clubmans 499cc, 1960 (UK)

Collection The Barber Vintage Motorsports Museum

The top-of-the-line Clubman inspired the café-racer look of the 1960s with its clip-on handlebars and swept-back exhaust pipe. This model is fine for street riding, but is also capable of racing performance and comes in Clubmans' racing trim.

Norton Manx 498cc, 1962 (UK)

Collection The Barber Vintage Motorsports Museum

This is the final version of the legendary Manx production racer. From its debut in the 1927 Isle of Man event, the Norton was considered unapproachable on the racetrack.

Matchless G50 496cc, 1962 (UK)

Collection The Barber Vintage Motorsports Museum

The G50 was specifically designed to compete in 500cc class races. It was less powerful than machines like the Manx, but its success was attributed to its unusually low weight—290 pounds.

Indian Chief 1200cc, 1946 (USA)
Private Collection

The Indian Chief debuted in 1922, twenty-one years after the Springfield, Massachusetts, company produced the first Indian "motocycle." The new Indian entry was initially powered by a 61-cubic-inch side-valve V-twin, and within two years replaced the Powerplus as Indian's top-of-the-line model. By the time this 1946 example rolled off the production line, the Chief, which had started out as a larger, more powerful version of the popular 37-cubic-inch Indian Scout, had grown to a full 74 cubic inches. The Chief also went through numerous refinements in its design over the years, including the standout sweeping fenders seen on this bike.

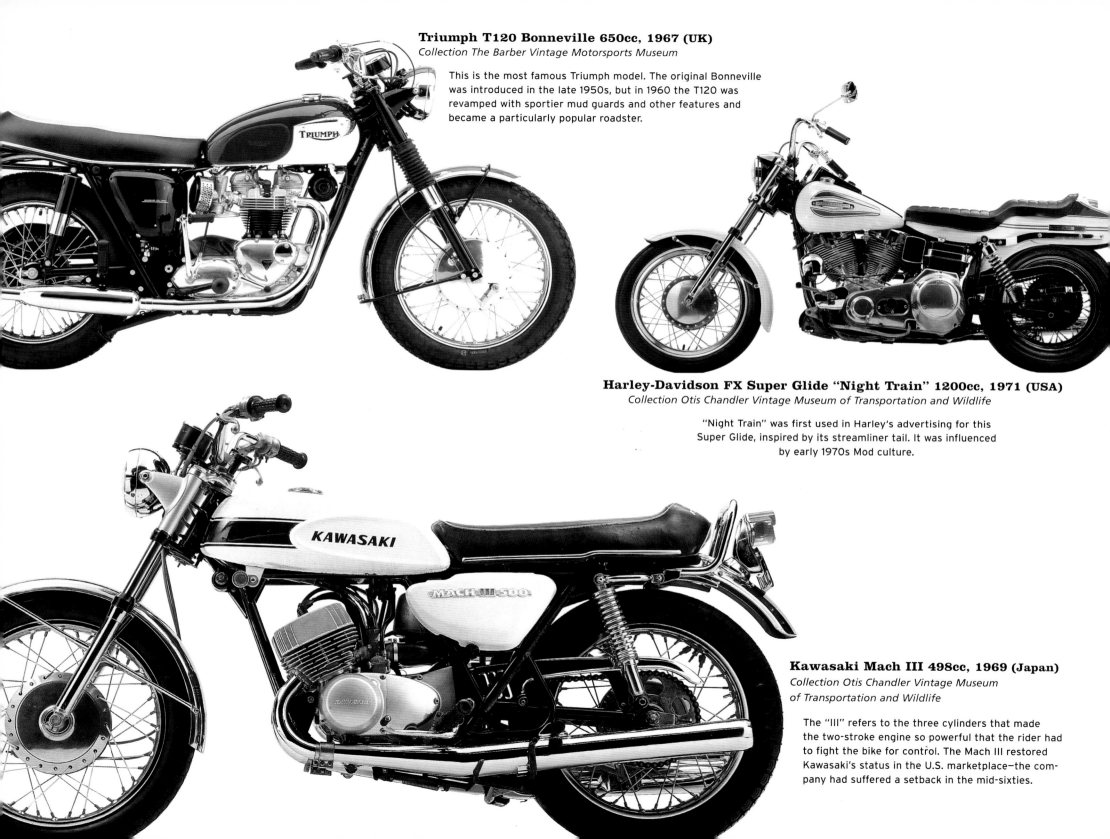

Triumph T120 Bonneville 650cc, 1967 (UK)
Collection The Barber Vintage Motorsports Museum

This is the most famous Triumph model. The original Bonneville was introduced in the late 1950s, but in 1960 the T120 was revamped with sportier mud guards and other features and became a particularly popular roadster.

Harley-Davidson FX Super Glide "Night Train" 1200cc, 1971 (USA)
Collection Otis Chandler Vintage Museum of Transportation and Wildlife

"Night Train" was first used in Harley's advertising for this Super Glide, inspired by its streamliner tail. It was influenced by early 1970s Mod culture.

Kawasaki Mach III 498cc, 1969 (Japan)
Collection Otis Chandler Vintage Museum of Transportation and Wildlife

The "III" refers to the three cylinders that made the two-stroke engine so powerful that the rider had to fight the bike for control. The Mach III restored Kawasaki's status in the U.S. marketplace—the company had suffered a setback in the mid-sixties.

Harley-Davidson XR750 750cc, 1972 (USA)

Collection Glenn M. Bator

This model has dominated dirt-track racing since the early 1970s, when the iron-barrelled engine was replaced by an aluminum V-twin design.

Harley-Davidson XLCR 1000cc, 1977 (USA)

Collection Otis Chandler Vintage Museum of Transportation and Wildlife

This was a radical design departure for Harley, as it was inspired by the lean lines of the European sportbike. The XLCR took Harley's usual market by surprise, as it was accustomed to stockier, low-to-the-ground bikes.

Triumph X75 Hurricane 750cc, 1973 (UK)

Collection The Barber Vintage Motorsports Museum

The movie *Easy Rider* had caused chopper mania in the USA; Triumph responded with this chopper-style triple. Availability was often limited to one per dealer.

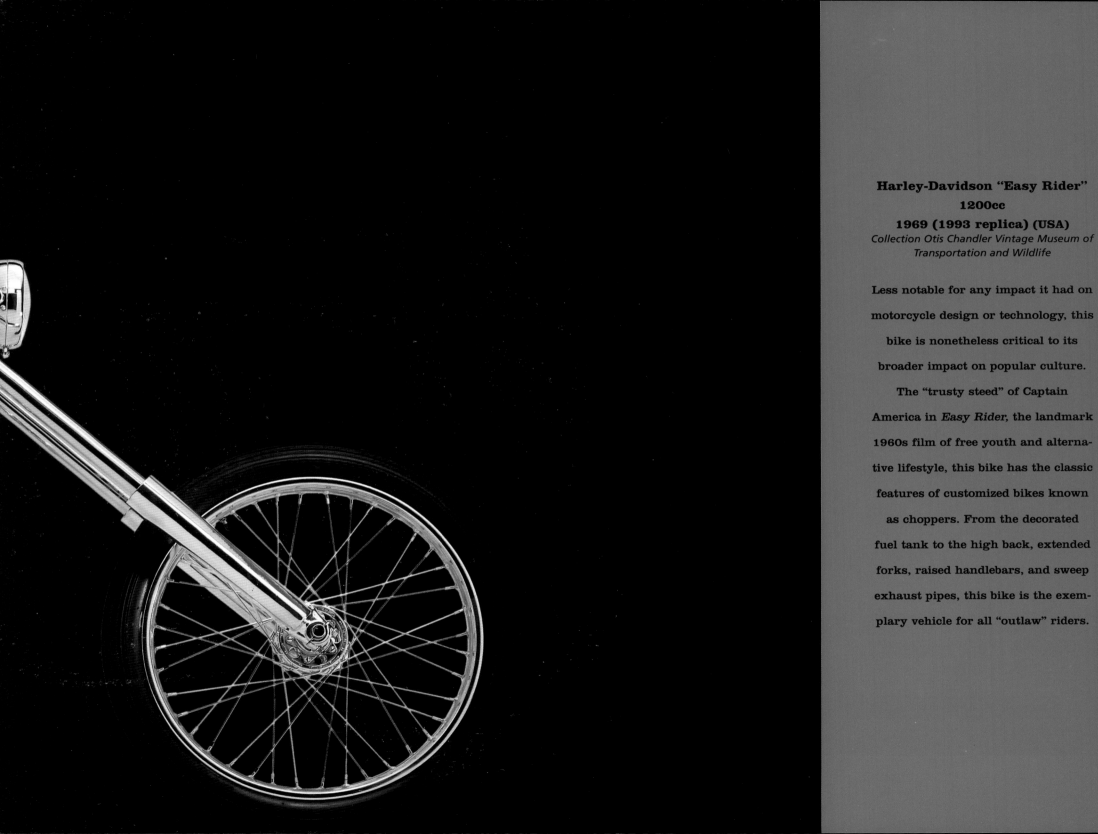

Harley-Davidson "Easy Rider"
1200cc
1969 (1993 replica) (USA)
Collection Otis Chandler Vintage Museum of
Transportation and Wildlife

Less notable for any impact it had on
motorcycle design or technology, this
bike is nonetheless critical to its
broader impact on popular culture.
The "trusty steed" of Captain
America in *Easy Rider*, the landmark
1960s film of free youth and alternative lifestyle, this bike has the classic
features of customized bikes known
as choppers. From the decorated
fuel tank to the high back, extended
forks, raised handlebars, and sweep
exhaust pipes, this bike is the exem-
plary vehicle for all "outlaw" riders.

Honda CB750K0 736cc
1970 (Japan)
Collection David Edwards

This motorcycle changed the course of history. Though Honda had been making bikes since the 1950s, this was its first large motorcycle, and it set the standard in the production of superbikes. Introduced in 1969, it was powered by Honda's new transverse-mounted, overhead-camshaft, in-line 750 four. The sophistication of the electric starter, a hydraulically operated disc brake, and inexpensive price presented a model that is still among the most popular today.

Suzuki Katana 997cc, 1982 (Japan)

Collection Otis Chandler Vintage Museum of Transportation and Wildlife

Turning to a former car designer, Suzuki wanted a new look for its bikes. The signature of Jan Fellstrom is the two-toned seat and integrated fuel tank.

Benelli Sei 906cc, 1984 (Italy)

Collection The Barber Vintage Motorsports Museum

The Sei was an attempt to compete with the Japanese, and the engine closely emulates Honda's 500cc models. An unusual feature is the twin-row rear chain.

Moto Guzzi 850 Le Mans 844cc, 1978 (Italy)

Collection The Barber Vintage Motorsports Museum

This is the original version of the Le Mans, one of the fastest Moto Guzzis designed. It is built low to the ground, but much of its weight was high enough in the frame to allow easy cornering.

Buell RS1200 1203cc, 1989 (USA)
Collection The Barber Vintage Motorsports Museum

Erik Buell, former racer and Harley-Davidson engineer, designed this roadster. The tubular steel frame holds the engine with an innovative rubber-mounting system.

Yamaha V-max 1198cc, 1989 (Japan)
Collection The Barber Vintage Motorsports Museum

The embellished styling of the V-max shows the influence of American customization. The mechanics, densely packed in the small frame, are topped by huge air intakes on the tank.

Aprilia Moto 6.5 649cc, 1995 (Italy)
Collection The Barber Vintage Motorsports Museum

Philippe Starck's design demonstrates the sensuous curves and whimsical lines that have made his furniture such a phenomenon. Moto hoped it would attract scooter riders usually intimidated by the sportbike.

Ducati 900 Monster 904cc
1997 (Italy)

Ducati began producing motorcycles in 1946, developing a reputation for powerful sportbikes. The Monster, somewhere between a racer and a cruiser and possessing the best qualities of both, created an overnight sensation. The frame is borrowed from Ducati race bikes, and its open architecture, tubular trellis frame, and rising-rate rear suspension are among its distinguishing features. Since its introduction in 1992, the 900 has become the bike of choice for many Grand Prix drivers.

Style Over Time
Motorcycle Aesthetics

In a motorcycle, form and function are inseparable: you cannot change one without considering the other. New developments in technology require new designs, and changes in taste and fashion often demand mechanical alterations.

In the early days, when motorcycles were more likely to be built in barns than factories, a handful of mavericks designed spontaneously, using whatever tenuous resources were available. Today engineering teams, bottom lines, and customer surveys call the aesthetic shots, but the individual fingerprints of the early designers are still visible in our modern machines.

As motorcycles grew in popularity, the pool of potential designers grew exponentially. Perhaps it is the relatively manageable size of a motorcycle, or the desire to push the envelope of the riding experience, that drives motorcycle owners to perpetually tinker with them, sometimes with innovative success and sometimes for the annals of oblivion.

By the time the motorcycle had become a permanent fixture on the American landscape, it was serving many needs. Suspension had evolved to serve the commuter and the racer alike. The main objective could be long-distance comfort or hugging the road for dear life.

Muddy rural roads helped riders flesh out the motorized bicycle with various fairings; racers looking for every inch of speed made these extensions aerodynamic and graceful. Now it's not uncommon to see not only permanent, integral fairing on a touring bike, but also built-in hard luggage.

Customizers took great pleasure in stripping down modern motorcycles that had, in their eyes, accumulated too many extraneous parts. They pushed some elements to outrageous extremes—apehanger handlebars or super-raked choppers, for example—proving that Darwinian practicality certainly did not apply to all motorcycle design.

Cruiser, sportbike, long-distance tourer, chopper, enduro: bikes today have evolved into many species, each design belying the rider's primary consideration—comfort, speed, looks, practicality, personal statement.

But function alone can't appeal to the soul. At best it soothes the need for rational answers and effective results. A well-functioning piece of machinery can be interesting but if it is too easily understood visually, the viewer quickly loses interest. However, a well functioning piece of machinery that has many facets—unexpected twists and shadows, proportions that defy physics and a gut-based appeal that borders on the primordial—is often elevated to a work of art.

It is this art, this mysterious marriage of form and function, that bears witness to the human need for flight—physical, mental, and spiritual. It holds beauty just beyond our grasp, and each new design, each new aesthetically superior machine, promises to take us just a little bit closer to that elusive state of grace.
DAVID ROBB

The use of wind tunnels has been essential to improving the aerodynamic performance of motorcycles, resulting in faster and sleeker machines.

I.D. Biker

by Melissa Holbrook Pierson

Among the most stereotyped characters ever to appear on the world stage is The Biker. He enters in a smear of black, a snarl ever-ready on his lips. A fearsome malefactor, his presence alone is a major crime. His bike is loud—boy, is it loud—and this is his hierarchy of concerns: 1. that assemblage of metal (don't breathe on its chrome); 2. his beer; 3. his buddies; . . . 8. his girlfriend. There the list ends. Even he can't quite remember what comes in between.

He is the actor recently portrayed in a painting titled *The Brotherhood* on a gold-rimmed porcelain collector plate, in which our chopper-riding hero, lightning shearing the dark sky behind, is watched over by his legendary predecessors: a mountain man, a Viking, a medieval knight, a pirate, and a cowboy, all looking suspiciously just like the biker. A cooler appreciation for history would yield proof that these archetypes actually share little, and hardly the same mustache, but when it comes to biking it's hard to keep a good bromide down.

The thing about these stereotypes—by definition "oversimplified opinions, affective attitudes, or uncritical judgments"—is that they only exist for those who are witless enough actually to believe that those biker exploitation flicks (*Hell's Belles*, *Born Losers*) tell some essential truth about people who like to ride motorcycles.

"Me and my 'buddy gal'—seeing sights—riding together on the finest motorcycle ever to hit the road . . . the Harley-Davidson 74 OHV.

Fellas, there is no greater thrill" is the slogan printed on the reverse of this 1954 Harley-Davidson factory advertising card.

The persistence of the myth of the bad-ass biker is something you live with, even though evidence to the contrary mounts; even though you know from experience that, say, every other motorcyclist you meet seems to be a photographer or civil engineer or systems analyst. (What is it about these professions?) A few years ago a survey commissioned by the Motorcycle Industry Council revealed a composite portrait of your usual biker: early thirties, married, college-educated, and earning just above the national median. White-, blue-, and gray-collar workers are evenly represented. By the way, he's a he—women still make up only a fraction of the ranks—but they say this is changing, and while they've been saying so for a very long while, it actually might be true of late.

But this is the stuff you feed to the outsiders, the doubters, the weak thinkers who don't see with their own eyes but rather with those of cultural cliché. You deplore their discrimination against the group: you, after all, are an individual!

Then you go out for a ride, and when you meet up with your cohorts of the open road, you make some very fussy typologies of your own.

Such highly scientific road polling (the clinical term is "checking people out") is carried out by most motorcyclists, who are members of one of the most divisive brotherhoods around. They just won't always admit it. Let us start at the top— or the middle or the bottom, depending on your personal prejudice.

Harley-Davidson is, by marketing design, diluting its aficionado base by selling more and more to RUBs–rich urban bikers. Thus the Milwaukee product is far less likely these days to be ridden by unemployed tool-and-die makers who sport large beer guts and belong to clubs whose membership requirement is an unkempt beard and black leather vest. Now the beard, if there is one, is trimmed, but you can never tell who it might be underneath that Harley™ vest: Soap opera actress? Congressman? Real estate baron? Or possibly it is an unemployed factory worker, whose lovingly kept old Low Rider would be worth a year's salary except that he won't sell at any price. That is the single glue that binds all the "My Iron Is Made in the USA" folks: loyalty to the brand. Whether there is something about the big Twins or just about the big Twins' marketing division, their riders rarely have eyes for anything else.

Road I.D.: Decked out in only the finest–concept suit, systems helmet, and spotless bike–the upright BMW motorcyclist is the polar opposite of the laid-back, helmetless Harley rider, outfitted in leather chaps for the long haul on his FXLR Low Rider.

Not so your typical vintage bike lover, promiscuous soul. So long as it was made before 1965, requires encyclopedic knowledge of Lucas electrics in order to turn over and/or stay running for four and a half minutes, and is in need of just that one original side cover before it can be called fully restored, it is a motorcycle that will receive a lustful lookover from one of these fanatics. He is likely to be young, well educated, and a computer graphics designer who sidelines in a rockabilly band. He started with one BSA Gold Star and now stores fourteen old carcasses—from BMW to Vespa—in a friend's garage. When he gets older, he will decide to go racing on his Velocette at Steamboat Springs just to see what it feels like. He won't care if he wins, because the experience is everything. And because he's too nice a guy to care about something so temporary.

The core of every urban biker teen's environment screams on summer nights with the sound of a Yamahonzuki being throttled to death (oh, would that it were so, that the rev limiter would break just this once). These flashily painted superbikes, with full fairings, fat, sticky tires, and ability to wheelie away and then make a mockery of twice the legal speed limit, are being used to ride up and down the block to keep the neighbors awake. They are a relatively cheap thrill, thanks to Japanese mass-production technology and easy payment plans, but they are more sophisticated—frighteningly so, in fact—than motorcyclists of twenty or thirty years ago could ever have dreamed. That is why they also appeal to the urban teen's opposite number: the serious speed freak. This girl knows what she wants and she's out to get it, wearing one-piece leathers and the full-face helmet her urban antagonist uses solely as a sop to the law, perched on top of his head like a full pan of Jiffy Pop.

The high-end speed freak, the kind who wouldn't be caught dead on a machine with such wide appeal, is these days heading straight for Ducati, which is fashioning itself a Bulgari among zircon purveyors. If you're a famous chef or a museum curator, the accessory of the moment is a hellfire-red 916; they're rare enough you won't see yourself coming and going, except when passing that famous litigator who just entered his second childhood. The beautiful sound Ducati is known for will announce to all your definite arrival, and the exquisite and quintessentially Italian craftsmanship tells anyone who stops to admire it outside the burg's hottest bistro that you are someone for whom the sensual pleasures are the only ones that count.

Neon lights turn to trails as Yamaha V-maxs scream down mean streets. Motorcycles are distinguished by their exhaust note: performance riders are drawn to the shrill cry of a four-cylinder engine, while traditionalists and old-timers tout the loping cadence of a large-displacement V-twin.

For the BMW rider, it's the going—and going and going—that matters most. As a group, they can claim the motorcycling world's highest literacy rates, but "fancy" is not their favorite word. The Beemers tally up their road miles in the thousands, and you can't do that without seriously scuffing your leathers and permanently marring the surface of your helmet with bug guts. BMW is the bike of choice for those who plan to ride down the African coast, compete in the Iron Butt, and keep the same scoot for at least twenty years. Sensible? Yes. And no. It's how they keep you guessing that makes these high-mileage free-thinkers more interesting in the aggregate than their relatively unexciting mounts would suggest.

The motorcycle you choose—cruiser or sportbike, import or domestic, museum piece or latest toy—is thus as specific a code as the clothes you wear. Yet there is only one thing that makes a "real" biker, and it isn't what marque you prefer. It's whether you give "The Wave" to every rider you pass.

This is because motorcyclists share a stronger secret bond than any spurious historicizing can ever forge: pound for pound, they are the nicest folk on the planet. Nice—yech, huh?

Don't let it get around. . . .

It will positively ruin your image.

A biker astride a classic Indian "motocycle" wearing vintage gear to match—a '50s cap with visor and gauntlet gloves.

Arlen Ness' chopped-down lowrider ready for action.

When Brand New

by Timothy Remus

Just Isn't Good Enough

Customizing is really nothing more than modifying a machine to suit better the taste of the owner. As such, motorcycle riders have been "customizing" their machines from day one, partly out of necessity and partly out of desire. Early riders individualized their Indians, Popes, and Merkels with windshields and leather bags simply as a way to make their machines more useful as everyday transportation. More involved with their machine—then and now—than a typical car driver, motorcycle riders are always quick to discover flaws in a factory design, to eliminate the weaknesses, and to improve the machine.

The ranks of motorcycling swelled after World War II, as American GIs returned home and bought motorcycles for quick, easy, and cheap transportation, often the same bikes they saw during their time in Europe. Many of those early Triumphs, BSAs, and Royal Enfields were customized with the addition of a smaller gas tank, smaller seat, and a Bates headlight. Harley-Davidson riders did very similar things to their bikes. The idea was to simplify the bike, to eliminate anything that wasn't necessary, and to replace any necessary features, such as handlebars, with more stylish implements.

People started to call the modified bikes "choppers," motorcycles stripped to their bare mechanical essentials. Starting in about 1969, the chopper craze ran like a freight train through the ranks of motorcycling. Propelled by the movie *Easy Rider*, choppers became a national and international phenomenon. Though the bikes we remember best might be Harley-Davidson Panheads with long, long front forks, wild paint detailing, and tall ape-hanger handlebars, plenty of Hondas, Kawasakis, and Triumphs were chopped as well—given longer forks, taller bars, and a Maltese-Cross mirror.

Detail of a classic frame motif—flames designed by Arlen Ness—on the gas tank of a chopper.

There is still a strong demand for choppers today, particularly retro choppers with modern Harley-Davidson V-twin engines and billet aluminum accessories, painted with candy hues so bright they hurt your eyes when viewed in the sun. The Harley-Davidson craze is so intense people wait for two to three years to get the bike of their dreams. For many owners, the customizing starts as soon as the new bike arrives. Both Harley-Davidson and a variety of aftermarket companies provide a bewildering array of parts intended to answer the rider's need for more style and color, everything from swoopy fender designs and long stretched gas tanks to chrome-plated trinkets and baubles. Rare is the owner who can resist the temptation to *improve* that new bike. While most of this customizing is done at home, some owners simply ship the complete machine to an outside shop. Well-known customizers, such as Donnie Smith or Arlen Ness, will transform your stock motorcycle into a longer, lower, brighter, and faster machine.

Current trends in customizing break down into two categories: fresh paint jobs accented by billet aluminum accessories, to improve the bike's aesthetics; or new carburetors, camshafts, and exhaust pipes, to give the bike more snort when the light turns green. As motorcycles wear their mechanical underpinnings out in the open for everyone to see, upgrades to carburetors, air cleaners, and brakes are visible to anyone with the curiosity to look. What would be a strictly mechanical improvement for a four-wheeler quickly becomes part of the aesthetic package for a motorcycle.

Some improvements walk a fine line between form and function. Four-piston front-brake calipers, carved from billet aluminum and chrome-plated to a high luster, provide a dramatic improvement in braking ability. Mounted to the front forks, a pair of these gleaming calipers also adds to the machine's visual pizzazz while making a subtle statement about the owner's good taste.

Riders of sportbikes, or "crotch rockets," are no different in their desire for a personalized machine, but the sport rider emphasizes function rather than form. Unlike the heavyweight cruisers from Milwaukee, sportbikes start life as fast, lightweight missiles. Improvements follow that same theme. Stock exhaust systems quickly give way to aluminum and carbon-fiber replacements, each five pounds lighter than the stock components. Two-up seats come off, to be replaced by solo mounts; suspension components are swapped for expensive, premium-grade replacements. Horsepower, already well over 100 on many of the large-displacement sportbikes, can be increased 10 or 20 percent with a change in carburetors and camshafts, or boosted to stratospheric levels with the addition of a turbocharger. How about a 500-pound machine with well over 200 horsepower easily capable of traveling at over 200 mph?

(top left) One of the favored routes taken by early customizers was to exaggerate by extension, sometimes resulting in choppers that spanned fifteen feet from the far edge of their skinny front tires back to the sky-grasping tip of their chromed "sissy bars." (right) The competition for individuality starts in the parking lot, as illustrated by this lineup of customized chopped bikes. (bottom left) A spectacular chopper—a pairing of Harley parts with a Jammer springer fork, a Paughco tank, and ape-hanger handlebars—built by Dave Royal.

A page from Donnie Smith's sketchbook showing a custom frame.

Front fork and custom brake caliper and polished brake rotor commonly seen on current custom Harley-Davidsons by Arlen Ness.

Arlen Ness-designed Sportster engine with chrome-plated rocker boxes.

Etched patterns grace the otherwise industrial-looking SU carburetor on a Harley-Davidson blower bike, designed by Al Reichenbach.

Motorcycles, and Harley-Davidsons in particular, have been called "rolling billboards," ones that each rider paints to suit individual taste. America's best-known customizer, Arlen Ness, explains, "A bike is a reflection of your personality, you don't want it looking like everyone else's. This is a hobby for most of these people. It's something they take pride in. Not like the everyday car they go to work in. They like it when people admire their work."

If Harley riders are hooked on style, sport riders have a corresponding need for speed. "I think the American male gets bored easily," Terry Kizer, better known as "Mr. Turbo" adds. "Our customers start with an 1100cc bike that's very fast just the way it comes from the factory. But after six months it doesn't provide the rider with the same adrenaline rush. That's when they bring it to us. We can literally double the horsepower or even triple it. That gets the old adrenaline pumping again."

Harley-Davidson riders customize a new motorcycle, one most people would find beautiful, just because they don't want to see ten bikes like theirs in the parking lot. Sport riders start with machines that are among the fastest street legal vehicles ever built and add even more horsepower in the apparent belief that a little too much is just enough. Though the machines have changed from those first single-cylinder bikes offered for sale early in the century, the riders apparently have not. No matter how good, how stylish, or how fast a new bike is, it's just never quite stylish or fast enough for a certain hardcore group of riders.

Arlen Ness is synonymous with the ultimate in customization. An artist with a unique vision, his paints come in candy-apple reds and greens and his canvas is the open road. From his home base in San Francisco the self-taught Ness has built an empire of fantasy machines for lucky customers with deep pockets. The center bike above, called the Smooth-Ness, was inspired by the Bugatti automobile of the Art Deco era and fetches $100,000. Pictured to each side of the Smooth-Ness is the Aero. Despite their museum quality, both bikes are completely ridable.

Ross Langlitz wearing a prototype design of his "classic" jacket, while astride a 1947 KSS 350 Velocette. This design includes a thick collar providing additional warmth.

by Marc Cook

Riding  Gear

Motorcycle apparel has always served two masters. One, predictably, is protection. What the rider wears should protect him in the event of an unplanned encounter with the terrain, make him comfortable in cold weather as well as hot, and provide relief from the elements. An apparel set, which includes a jacket or suit, helmet, gloves, and special boots, should as a whole safeguard the rider from rain, road rash, and environmental discomfort. "A second skin" is how many think of it. Wearing his protective Langlitz jacket, a rider who dumped his Harley at 50 mph reported that he felt like he was simply "sliding into first base."

Bike apparel's second dictate is style. Today's riders are as fashion-conscious as any Gen Xer. A traditional Harley rider wants a black leather jacket that is somewhere between the pattern of a World War II bomber jacket and what Marlon Brando wore in 1954's *The Wild One*. (Never mind that Brando's mount was a Triumph, not a Harley.) Owners of ultra-sporting models yearn for full leather suits patterned after successful race bike riders, oftentimes in garish colors and frequently splashed with corporate signage. Sport-touring riders—those who like to combine the long-distance journeys of a touring rider with some measure of over-the-road speed—tend toward hybrid outfits that combine the pure functionality of a racing suit with convenience items, like generous pockets and flexible layering.

Motorcycle apparel quickly developed from more pedestrian roots. Long coats, "dusters," and other protective attire designed for activities such as horseback riding carried significant shortcomings. The great difference in the speed of a motorcycle compared to that of a horse, even at the turn of the century, accentuated the limitations of the early gear. A swift fall from a motorcycle would shred clothing, and the loose construction of livery wear offered no protection from the hurricane-like winds a bike's velocity created.

The Motorcyclist's Tailor

Ross Langlitz, founder of Langlitz Leathers (originally named Speedway Togs) in Portland, Oregon, lost his right leg in a motorcycle accident when he was 17, but still went on to win 47 racing trophies from 1938 to 1954. A glove cutter, he turned to "building" jackets in 1947. Finding aviator gear too bulky and airy for bike riding, he added long zippered sleeves, wind-protection collars and waistbands, and an offset zipper with an overlap to protect the rider's front. Langlitz leathers are still all custom made, focusing on durability and protection. Tales of cyclists in accidents refusing to let paramedics cut jackets or pants to free their limbs are part and parcel of cycle lore. "I've seen guys sit up and wiggle broken legs out of their Western Langlitzes," said one rider speaking for all who protect their thick leathers.

The dress collar provides the traditional biker look. An optional fur piece can be snapped over the collar for warmth in the chill of winter.

Thick protective water-resistant leather functions as an outer skin, saving the biker's real hide in the event of an accident.

The durable, heavy-duty, luggage-type brass zipper in front is offset with an overlap that keeps out wind and rain.

Lots of pockets (most zippered) give easy access to gloves, keys, maps, and wallets.

Long, zippered sleeves keep the jacket warm and airtight.

The waistband dips in the rear to protect the small of the back in a lean-forward riding position. The reinforced band is like a truss. It gives the rider more protection from road shock.

The Columbia jacket, a classic that has stood the test of time. Ross Langlitz's design—an evolution from the less practical leather jackets available to bikers in the 1940s—has become an industry standard.

Form follows function in the BMW Kalahari jacket. Today's trend in modern motorcyclist clothing design is the use of such new tear-resistant and waterproof materials as cordura and Gore-Tex®, which breathe better than leather, and release body moisture for maximum comfort. Removable shoulder and elbow pads and a spine protector with additional layers of Kevlar® fabric provide top-notch protection in a fall.

The Hells Angels "outlaw" look has been appropriated even by riders with no club connection. "Colors" (a patch sewn on the back of riding gear to identify an "outlaw" group) have now taken on much tamer overtones and have been coopted into the motorcycle mainstream.

In the absence of man-made materials suitable for motorcycling, leather dominated. Jackets, pants, vests (for summer wear), and chaps—a sort of cutout version of pants designed to protect the front of the rider's legs and hips—all were made from various grades and thicknesses of leather. But leather neither breathes well—a good thing for staving off chills on a cold winter night, but not so good for summer riding—nor is it inherently waterproof. A sopping-wet leather jacket takes on considerable liquid weight.

In the wet-weather countries of northern Europe, the waxed-cotton jacket became a riding staple. This durable garment, still in production, combines the flexibility of a fabric-based suit with water repellency. But additional layers of material were needed to match leather's outstanding abrasion resistance. By the 1960s miracle synthetic fabrics came to motorcycling that provided good insulation, reasonable crash protection, and some flexibility in manufacturing. Nevertheless, the leather jacket—which also has the great attraction of molding itself over time into the wearer's shape—has prevailed as the rider's choice, an issue now as much of style as protection.

(far left) 1975 Vanson Leathers racing suit, which has been track-tested countless times. Most full race suits are custom-made and designed to combine freedom of movement for racers and protection in the event of a crash. (left) Aerostich's Roadcrafter suit's innovative design, with a continuous zipper from collar to ankle, makes it easy to put on over street clothes. This clothing manufacturer has been a pioneer in using man-made materials for motorcycle gear.

Decked out in protective racing attire, the road racer's extreme lean angle causes a knee to come into contact with the ground when cornering.

Today's race suits, made of conventional leather whose main strength is its abrasion resistance, have extremely sophisticated protective features, including plastic and foam pads for the elbows, shoulders, and back, as well as removable Velcro knee pads that grind down during cornering. The anatomically shaped body armor is an essential protective part of a race suit.

Italy's Luca Cadalora speeds to the finish, marking the first win for Marlboro Yamaha at the U.S. Grand Prix. Today's racer—and machine—are turned into moving billboards, clad head to toe in gear emblazoned with sponsors' logos.

Boots and gloves, other essential elements of a rider's kit, have evolved from humble origins in work gloves and work boots to today's dedicated motorcycle apparel that reflects the particular needs of the rider. Extensive study of motorcycle accidents, both on the road and at the racetrack, has given garment makers the full picture of how to cocoon a rider. Gloves, for example, are built with additional padding atop the fingers—to prevent car-launched road hazards from creating injuries—and special wear-resistant materials in the heel of the palm. Moreover, good glove-makers are careful to limit (or eliminate) seams in the palm of the hand so that the rider's connection with the bike's throttle is not filtered or compromised. Modern boots combine thick, grip-laden soles with a boot-upper construction that allows freedom of movement.

Boots are also matched to a bike's use and specialization. Lightweight boots and gloves for racing increase the rider's ability to move around on the bike, optimizing the critical transfers of weight needed for cornering, while touring riders prefer heavier boots that will help them steady 700-pound machines and keep their feet warm on long rides. Some urban riders often seem more concerned how the boots look while they're strolling around coffee shops than in the boots' over-the-road abilities. To be prepared for all occasions, most longtime riders have several sets of boots and gloves, suitable for the ride's occasion and scope.

(left) Modern gloves are made of a combination of advanced materials—nylon, Kevlar®, and leather. They provide more protection and flexibility than old general-purpose gloves. (near left) Racer David Aldana wore these bone gloves (part of a whole skeletal suit) for Vanson Leathers, evoking the death-defying nature of racing. (middle) Elkskin work gloves will do the job but are not optimized for motorcycling. (near right, right) Contemporary leather boots illustrate the protective qualities of today's new materials. Kevlar® reinforcements provide stability and impact resistance. Shin plates protect shins from debris. Motorcycle boots are made of sturdy, water-repellent leather. Their non-slip rubber soles are oil resistant. Both pairs of boots are too bulky for racers.

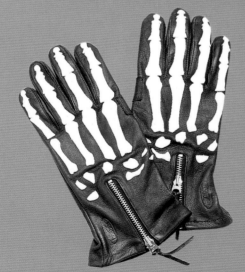
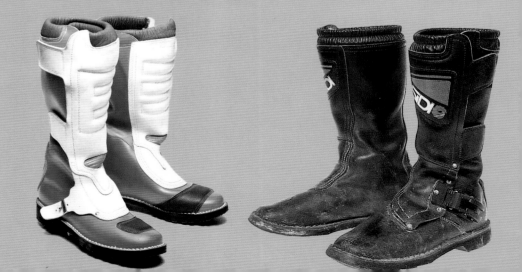

MECO MOTORCYCLE SUITS

The coat as shown in cut is the long Norfolk style which is roomy and fits well, and keeps its shape. The best of workmanship has been put in them. The edges are faced back 4 in. The three pockets have snap buttons covered to match the cloth, and each is reinforced at the edges. Presto collar that buttons tight about the neck when riding in dust, or turns down neatly when desired. Sleeves have button flap to button tight about the wrist to keep out the dust. This is absolutely the best made garment we can procure. There is a vast difference in the style and makeup of this coat than in many offered for sale. Every convenience for the rider has been incorporated in it.

The trousers, as shown in cut, are made full peg top so they will be roomy and comfortable about the hips and knees. Below the knees they lace around the calf snugly and extend only to the shoe tops so leggins can be worn without having to fold the cloth around the ankle. The cut is very stylish. The two hip and watch pockets have buttoned flaps, the two side pockets are extra deep. Belt straps and inside suspender buttons are provided. Seams are double stitched. The inside of the tops are nicely faced. Each have double seat for long service. The trousers have a style and fit about them that cannot be duplicated.

YOUR MONEY BACK, if on examining them you do not find they are absolutely just what you want.

MECO WHIPCORD SUITS—Either Brown or Salt and Pepper.

Either of these suits are very dressy and will please the most fastidious rider. The colors are not conspicuous and they always look dressy. *It is a matter of taste* between the dark Brown or the Salt and Pepper. Either make an ideal Touring Suit that will not readily show dirt and can be comfortably worn when away from the Motorcycle. This well known Whipcord material is the best wearing fabric made for this purpose. When ordering specify size and color wished.

MECO KHAKI SUIT—Olive Green.

This is a very serviceable cloth that for all around use cannot be equalled. It is a trifle lighter in weight than the Whipcord, but plenty heavy for Summer riding. Dust and grease do not readily show and the color is just the right shade to make a classy suit. It will give long service, hold its color and shape and you will like it far better than the ordinary Khaki colors.

Always state size; For trousers—measure loosely around the waist. For Coat—measure loosely.

Caps to Match MECO Suits

This cap can be supplied to match either the SALT AND PEPPER—the BROWN—or the KHAKI Suits.

They are made of the same material as the different suits and when used with any of the above suits, make a very attractive outfit. They are well made and nicely lined. On account of the high grade material and workmanship, they will give long service.

As shown in cut they are made with ear and neck shield. The fore-piece is set to permit the wearing of goggles without discomfort. When ordering, specify color and give size.

Black Leather Cap

This is our popular Leather Motorcycle Cap of which we have sold hundreds. The quality is equal to the highest priced Cap on the market. It is made of dull finished, soft, black leather and nicely lined with silkiline. *Give size when ordering.*

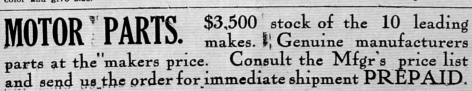
Royal Tourists Cap

This water-proof, light-weight cap has the advantage over others in that the goggles are attached to the cap, where they cannot be lost or easily broken. The combination also makes a better fitting goggle that does away with eye-strain on long trips.

Our illustration shows the goggle, fore-piece and ear-muffs turned up as each would be carried when not in use. When goggles are in use the fore-piece is to be turned up behind and visa-versa. Very handy when goggles are wanted and out of the way when not wanted.

The quality is the best obtainable. The color is the newest popular shade of Dark Olive Grey, hard finished worsted. The collapsible goggles are the best quality and bound with chenille. For a touring or speed cap it cannot be duplicated in usefulness, quality or price. *Give size when ordering.*

Haupt Cap

Made of medium weight Dark Grey Felt. Has dust protectors or ear muffs which can be fastened up or down. It has a short close fitting fore piece silk lined. This Cap is light weight for summer riding. Sits lightly on the head and yet cannot be blown off. Be sure and add one to your spring order. Because the price is low do not mistake this for the cheap caps so often sold at our price. *Give size when ordering.*

Thomas Cap

This serviceable Cap is made of coarse weave mixed grey cloth. It has a short, close fitting forepiece so well liked by the riders. The Ear Muffs extend around the back and are fastened up with a patent snap. When Muff is down it fastens under the chin with an elastic band. This Cap is heavier than others we list and can be used for Fall and Spring riding. It is silk lined and the best quality. It is a decided bargain. *Give size when ordering.*

Heavy Kersey Cap

An extremely well-made cap. Dark in color, silk lined and durable cap for winter riding. It is about the same style as the Thomas, except that it has larger Ear-muffs which are fastened nearer the top of the cap or under the chin as desired. It will protect the head and ears in the coldest weather. *Give size when ordering.*

Gauntlet No. 11. *Black Only*

This Gauntlet as shown by the cut is extremely long. The cuff reaches nearly to the elbow and affords excellent protection to the sleeve. Made of light weight Reindeer, but on account of the high grade quality of this leather, it will give as much wear as the heavier gloves on the market. The cuff is lined with black silk and insures plenty of room for the coat sleeve. This cuff, while very large, is of the flexible folding style. The strap on wrist is adjustable. *Give size when ordering.*

Gauntlet No. 6. *Tan or Black*

Made of medium weight horse hide, stitched extra heavy and made for long wear. Has very neat appearance. The cuff has two straps and when opened up to the largest size measures 10½ inches across, giving plenty of room for the sleeve. This glove can be folded very small for carrying in pocket. You cannot afford to buy gloves elsewhere when we are offering a glove of this quality at so low a price. *Give size and color when ordering.*

Gauntlet No. 4. *Black Only*

This gauntlet is made of heavy weight horsehide and heavily stitched throughout. It is double thickness and double stitched at the base of the thumb where the wear comes and where so many gauntlets rip. Has a cord and patent clasp at the wrist so it can always be fitted. The cuff is extra heavy and measures 9½ inches across. *Give size when ordering.*

Gauntlet No. 1 B

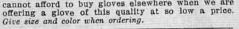

Made of extra heavy calf skin. The cuff as shown in the cut is shaped correctly for the coat sleeve. The cuff is canvas lined and 8½ inches across. It is made in every way for wear and when price is considered it is a great bargain. *Give size when ordering.*

Gauntlet No. 5
BLACK ONLY—FLEECE LINED. These are very durable and resembles No. 11 with wrist strap.

The canvas, cork, and leather of early helmets has been replaced today by such sturdy materials as fiberglass and reinforced plastic. Helmets are sacrificial: after a significant impact—whether from an accident or even from toppling off the top shelf in the garage—the helmet should be retired. (far left) The pudding bowl helmet is reminiscent of 1950s and 60s racers' helmets. (middle left) The classic open-face design is most often worn with goggles and remains popular with urban bikers. Helmets are made for specific types of riding. (middle right) This dirt-racing helmet features an extended protective visor, corporate logos, and colorful graphics. (far right) The full-face helmet provides maximum protection and an integral face shield. Vents allow airflow; with thanks to wind-tunnel research, the helmet's aerodynamics have been engineered to reduce wind noise.

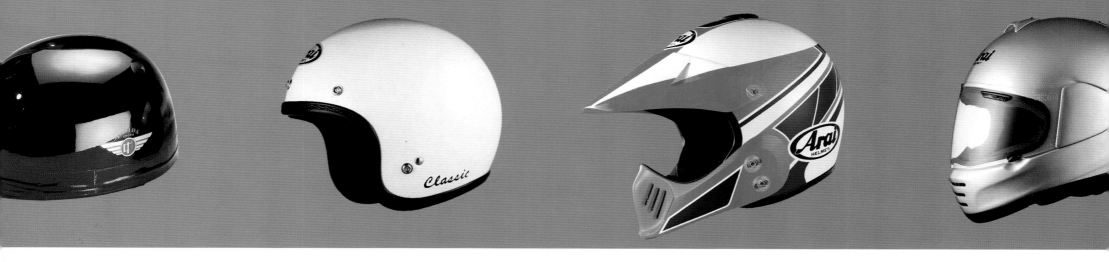

No other item in motorcycling has raised so much controversy as the helmet, thanks in part to laws enacted in several states in the early 1960s mandating helmet use—a tremendously unpopular requirement. At first, there was no such thing as a protective helmet, although early riders wore various hats and leather hoods for comfort, as well as goggles for eye protection. In time, as the severity of head injuries tracked the increase in speed of motorcycles, the use of helmets grew. But pioneering motorcycle helmets were good for little more than abrasion protection. In addition, early helmet designs covered only the crown of the head, thus offering no protection to the face, ears, or neck.

As open-face helmets—universally popular—eventually evolved into full-face designs by the late 1960s so too did the construction materials evolve. Plain fiberglass construction gave way to hybrids, with layers of ballistic Kevlar® and ultra-light (and ultra-strong) carbon fiber to save weight. These helmets are wind-tunnel–tested to cut wind noise. Even with air vents for comfort and scratch- and glare-proof visors to shield the eyes, many riders in warmer climes prefer open-faced helmets. Advances in high-density foam liners have allowed helmet designers to tailor the material's characteristics so that the helmet crushes in just the right way, properly absorbing impact forces.

Despite the current preference for "classic" motorcycles, and the enormous popularity of stylish vintage clothing (desired as much by many who've never even been a biker), riders today still appreciate the technological advances in composites, fabrics, and computer-aided manufacturing that have made their attire far more functional, useful, and comfortable.

The **Fashionable** **Motorcycle** *Look*

The leather motorcycle jacket arrived in high fashion on the backs of off-duty models, natural trophies to the men who might feign to drive motorcycles. Fashion observed its models coming to the dressing room in a street style that could quickly and earnestly be translated into high style. And, like the T-shirt, the motorcycle jacket never loses its identity in fashion: it can become menswear or womenswear, sportswear or even eveningwear, yet always retains its personality. That is the true strength of the motorcycle jacket. Its leather and its silhouette (a V-shape that is ideal for men or women) remain the same. Even if Donna Karan employs it in coordinated luxury with cashmere for so-called basic black or Gianni Versace embellishes it with more ornamentation than skid-protective patches, the motorcycle jacket still has the legend of the road, the scent of masculinity, and the aura of the invincible.

While weather-protective leather—often associated with valor—had entered fashion in the 1910s in the form of the aviator jacket, Americans of the post-World War II interstate age related less to the aviator heroes of the past and rallied around the new individualist hero—the motorcycle rider. The

tough skin and male silhouette of a leather jacket's expansive chest and narrowed waist could also be bestowed by any Sir Raleigh of the road on women needing warmth or protection.

But if the leather jacket's road-warrior beginnings cannot be erased, fashion and popular culture have acted to supplement its decoration. In the 1950s individual names and club identities were added to the jackets, in a working-class style. Rock music introduced leather jackets that showed off the bodies of male performers Elvis Presley, Mick Jagger, David Bowie, Sid Vicious, and Michael Jackson. If popular culture could augment individual identity, then fashion could readily do the same, inviting the interests of Jean-Paul Gaultier, Calugi e Giannelli, Claude Montana, and other "street"-savvy designers who individualized the garment. For female performers such as Cher, Madonna, and Tina Turner, the motorcycle jacket connotes both power and personality. Rock put the motorcycle jacket and boots into the spotlight, and the fashion runway was not far behind.

RICHARD MARTIN

(top) At the other end of the fashion spectrum, a couple at the Sturgis rally strut their homemade stuff.

(bottom) Gianni Versace's studded black leather and silk crepe ensemble (fall/winter 1991-92), embellished with silver- and gold-tone metal studs.

(left) Borrowing the old nickname of a Harley-Davidson bike—"hog"—as their acronym, H.O.G. (Harley Owners Group) represents a diverse constituency of riders. (right) The annual bike races at Daytona Beach, Florida, began originally on the vast strip of sand in 1937 (as seen here at the 1947 race). Since that date, the Daytona races have graduated to the status of a professional event with a track built to code. Daytona provides standards that racing clubs follow.

Clubs  Associations

by John Carroll

Motorcycling has always been a social activity, even when the machine was little more than a pedal bicycle with a small engine attached. People riding the newfangled contraptions were happy to see fellow riders on the road, and they often stopped to greet each other. It wasn't long before riders were going on runs together; then, in the early 1900s, racing started to take off on U.S. board and dirt tracks. Early board racers, who competed on elliptical tracks made of timber, were viewed as daredevils on wheels.

In 1903 the Federation of American Motorcyclists (FAM), an organization which regulated sporting activities, was established. In 1912, FAM held a convention in Denver, Colorado—one of the first official motorcycle gatherings. Riders braved bad weather and muddy midwestern roads to be there. Concurrent with the growth of the motorcycle industry, racing and social clubs were formed. Support from motorcycle companies for racing was strong since race wins boosted sales. Thus ardent brand identity, which endures to this day, became associated with motorcycle culture.

By the 1920s the motorcycle became a practical means of mass transportation. In the 1930s national concrete track racing—which replaced the outmoded board tracks—and other events, such as hill climbs and long-distance touring, emerged throughout the country. Manufacturers participated directly. In 1935, Harley-Davidson founder Walter Davidson won the Cow Bell Classic—an event like today's Enduro—so-called because the winner's name was inscribed on an old cow bell. In 1937, in Sturgis, South Dakota, Indian dealer Pappy Hoel and his club, The Jackpine Gypsies, began throwing an annual picnic and hill climb for customers. This picnic has evolved into one of the largest rallies in the U.S. today, the Black Hills Classic. At Daytona, the American Motorcycle Association (AMA), anxious to reignite interest in motorcycling after the Depression, organized a 200-mile race on the beach, known today as the Daytona 200.

After World War II, veterans returned to the U.S. wanting more from motorcycling than dealer picnics. Many banded together in groups we know today as "outlaw" biker gangs—the Booze Fighters, the Galloping Gooses, and the Hells Angels. Hunter S. Thompson commented later that many small towns got their first taste of tourism not from families in cars, but boozing city boys on motorcycles.

On July 4, 1947, during the AMA-sponsored races in Hollister, California, some of the spectators from these clubs got rowdy, resulting in the AMA's denunciation of "outlaw" bikers. It was official—"them" against "us." The 1% (the AMA-ascribed number referring to the percentage of bikers that belong to this group) proudly wore a patch proclaiming that they were just that—"One-Percenters." Hells Angels, Outlaws, Satans Slaves, and others flew their colors with pride, relishing in their difference. Headlines and notoriety soon spread like bushfire. The AMA was caught off-guard, and other clubs tried to live down the image of the renegade biker.

While the 1% captured the attention of the media, times were good for motorcycling. By the late 1950s in the U.S., a British invasion had begun: Triumphs were winning races, and British bikes were attracting a loyal following due to their superior speed. Then the Japanese arrived. Hondas, Yamahas, and Kawasakis changed the face of motorcycling forever by bringing affordability and middle-class respectability to riding through such marketing campaigns as: "You meet the nicest people on a Honda."

Waves of imports eventually toppled Harley's dominance, but one type of rider stuck with it through good times and bad—the 1%. The Sons of Silence, The Pagans, Bandidos, and others flew their colors from behind the bars of a big Harley. Club rules: "A member must own a Harley-Davidson of more than 750cc capacity."

Great Britain has a distinct biker heritage of its own. Since the motorcycle's earliest days, there have been noted British manufacturers—companies such as BSA, which produced the basic machines on which men traveled to work. From these working-class roots came numerous fashions, not least of which was the 1950 rock 'n' roll–born Teddy Boys.

The Rockers also emerged at this time, riding the fast British street bikes and creating an identity that took cues from Brando's *The Wild One.* Rockers ruled London's North Circular from the saddles of Café Racers made by Triumph, Norton, and BSA. Cafés such as the Ace and The Busy Bee were popular with the "Ton-Up" boys, who would put a record on the jukebox and race around the block to be back before it finished playing. Later, around 1964, a different crowd adopted Italian motorscooters and a more modern style of clothing, calling themselves Mods.

The Vietnam War had a negative impact on the Asian invasion of motorcycles—sales dwindled. Harley fought back for a share of the market it had lost and was supported by bikers who had returned from Vietnam. Later they formed the Vietnam Veterans Motorcycle Club, donning a patch that made explicit what its members had done for America.

Harley also took a subtler path. In a play on the slang for a big bike, "hog," they formed the Harley Owners Group (H.O.G.) and sought to reclaim the family tradition of motorcycling. Not everybody agreed with this strategy: "If motorcycling was a family affair, Harleys would have four doors," remarked a biker at Sturgis.

Both H.O.G. and the Bros Club (formed by *Easyriders*, the magazine favored by renegade bikers) grew, as did other organizations dedicated to specific makes and models, including the BMW Motorcycle Owners Club and the Gold Wing Owners Association. Race events are conducted under the auspices of organizations such as the American Historic Racing Motorcycle Association (AHRMA). More specialized clubs have emerged to represent every social, political, or religious interest (Christian Motorcyclist Association, Tribe of Judea, and The God Squad). And women's clubs are on the rise (Women in the Wind, Women's International Motorcycle Association [WIMA], and Ebony Queens). There's even a club for law enforcement officers: Blue Knights International Law Enforcement.

In the 1990s motorcyling is enjoying an unprecedented renaissance. The 1% clubs thrive internationally despite attempts by law enforcement agencies to contain them. (The Hells Angels have clubs in London, Germany, Switzerland, Australia, and Canada.) Club members communicate via the Internet or specialty magazines, from as far away as Beijing to as close as down the street. In short, if it has two wheels, there's an organization for its enthusiasts.

NO SMOKING

The shock of the new from *I Love Lucy*: Ethel and Fred surprise neighbors Ricky and Lucy by opting for the economy of a motorcycle to go cross-country to Hollywood.

Mainstreaming *Bike Culture: Bikes 'R' Us*

by Ted Polhemus

It's the late 1950s. I'm about to become one of the first generation of "teenagers." The family is driving down Corlies Avenue in Neptune, New Jersey—this is the "bad" part of town, and there, outside the pool hall, are a dozen aliens from some strange planet. They're wearing black leather jackets with lots of zips and studs, lazing about with elegant studied casualness on their mean-looking motorcycles, and working gravity-defying cigarettes held up by a slight inclination of the lip. I'm fascinated by what I see—especially the girls in extra tight jeans, their hair twisted like exploding peroxide bombs. "Juvenile delinquents, a bunch of punks," my father sternly advises.

America *was* in the grip of moral panic. Back in 1947 a group of bikers had "invaded" the town of Hollister, California —an event which was first hyped in Frank Rooney's 1951 *Harper's* article "Cyclist Raid" and was immortalized in the 1953 film *The Wild One,* starring Marlon Brando. As the film's director, Stanley Kramer, would later comment, "We simply showed that this was the first indication that a whole set of people were going to divorce themselves from society and set up their own standards."

In fact there were other outsiders busy divorcing themselves from Eisenhower's America: the Beats and hipsters. But these bikers were tough and mean. And unlike the college-educated Beats, they were working-class. Every "respectable" parent in the country feared that their sons might become one of these motorized outlaws and that their daughters might go out with them.

But class barriers held strong. When the father of the protagonist of the Shangri-Las' 1965 song "Leader of the Pack" tells her to "find somebody new" from the "right part of town," she does what she is told. Likewise, the daughter of the police chief in *The Wild One* toyed with jumping on the back of Johnny's Triumph and roaring off into a more exciting life, but in the end she pulled back from the abyss.

Today the policeman's daughter rides her own big bad bike—maybe to the rallies at Sturgis or Daytona, where she can party with the modern-day equivalent of "Johnny" (who might be a Hells Angel or a stockbroker or movie star). Now families from my hometown can pop up to New York City for a meal at the Harley-Davidson Cafe (where even biker jackets for toddlers can be purchased) while would-be street-cred trendies can drink at the Hogs and Heifers bar.

How did bikes and bikers make it from being the most peripheral and feared of subcultures to being lauded as an art form in museums? How did "Bad" become a synonym for "Good" and the juvenile delinquent become the embodiment of that rugged individualism that previously was personified only by the cowboy in a white hat?

Until the end of the 1960s, the basically negative premise set down by *The Wild One* was perpetuated—that while bikers might be sexy and stylish, they are ultimately a bunch of confused, fatally flawed, psychologically dysfunctional losers who will never "get anywhere." We can see this in "biker exploitation" movies such as *Motorcycle Gang* (1957), *Hell's Angels on Wheels* (1967), or *The Hellcats* (1968), which emerged in the wake of *The Wild One*. Neither television (e.g., leather-jacket-clad James Dean in *I Am a Fool*, 1954) nor the print media ("California Takes Steps to Curb Terrorism of Ruffian Cyclists," *The New York Times,* 1965) could bring themselves to paint a more sympathetic picture of bikers—with only Hunter S. Thompson's 1966 *Hell's Angels* (a gut-wrenching inside look at the most notorious "outlaw" biker group) mixing respect with trepidation.

A second phase ran from the early 1960s through the 1970s, when bikers came into conflict with subsequent youth cultures. Bikers were inevitably the guys in black—the rebellious, less attractive, and less penetrable alternative for youth. In Britain the rise of the Mods in the early 1960s presented the "Rockers" (as bikers were then called in the U.K.) with a new and far more ferocious enemy than mainstream society. Fashionable and futuristic, the Mods saw the Rockers as a Neanderthal anachronism that should be exterminated. As The Who's 1979 film *Quadrophenia* relives, they attempted to do just this in pitched battles at British seaside resorts throughout the summer of 1964. Rockers remained on the fringes while the extent of the Mod's success was evident in their domination of the new youth-oriented TV programs like *Ready! Steady! Go!*, in the popularity of Modish-groups like The Small Faces and The Who, and in the number of tourists flocking to their old stomping ground, London's Carnaby Street.

After *Easy Rider* our popular culture entered a stage in which bikes become covetable consumer icons and bikers become heroes. A plethora of popular American TV shows soon emerged in quick succession—the most obvious example being *Happy Days*. When it debuted in 1973 the Fonz was dressed in a pale blue nylon windbreaker, but soon the producers realized that the world was ready for a black-leather-clad hero.

At the same time fashion put biker imagery back onto the catwalk and our backs. There can be no doubt that the classic black leather motorcycle jacket has long had a formidable symbolic power. It was leather gear worn by pop star Gene Vincent on British TV and the "kinky" fashions of "Swinging London" (as seen in *The Avengers*) that initially brought this material within the sphere of popular culture (which is a bit ironic given Modish Britain's distaste for the leather-clad Rockers). Marianne Faithfull in the film *Girl on a Motorcycle* (released as *Naked Under Leather* in the U.S.) continued in the same sexy, sartorial vein. In America it was left to "Lizard King" Jim Morrison to show how men too could get into (and out of) leather. Another "King," Elvis, made use of the same garments for his 1968 comeback concert for NBC.

It was only in the 1980s that leather and, in particular, biker-style garments, entered the word of high fashion—and subsequently materialized at the local shopping mall. While once new fashions only trickled down from the rich to the not-so-rich, the 1980s saw a complete inversion: styles deemed "street credible" filtered up to influence even the most elite designers. And there is no more perfect example of this than how high-fashion designers reinvented (or, more frankly, ripped off) the biker's classic leather jacket. Montana, Mugler, Versace, Gaultier, and a host of others converted what had once been the most castigated of garments into the most coveted.

And thus we come full circle with those juvenile delinquents in their black leathers outside the pool hall now being sought after to model in *Vogue*.

("What are you rebelling against?")
("What have ya got?")

Well, not much really. You see, Johnny, you're one of us now.

(clockwise) **Elvis Presley** turns rough and tough into cool and sexy as a leather-clad rebel in the 1964 film *Roustabout*. Shiny leather-skinned **Marianne Faithfull** in the 1970 film *Girl on a Motorcycle* (released as *Naked Under Leather* in the U.S.). **Doors' lead singer Jim Morrison** as a "lounge lizard." **Supermodel Carla Bruni** donning outlaw chic by Claude Montana (fall/winter 1991-92). **Comedian Jay Leno** trades Hugo Boss for a leather jacket and he hits the streets.

The Motorcycle *On Screen*

by John G. Hanhardt

Racing across the screen and into our imagination, the motorcycle is best known as the protagonist of the 1960s biker genre pictures. But even this summary chronology shows that the story of the motorcycle and the movies is far more complex and varied. In films in which the motorcycle features prominently, the biker/hero manifests a desire to control his destiny and expresses his independence from the state, invoking heroic themes that have always been a part of the mythology of the American way of life.

Just as the silver screen gave us the cowboy riding his horse into the nineteenth-century sunset, the lone rider of the twentieth-century's mechanized bike was both a fearless and a vulnerable explorer, an independent hero who was confronted with problems he had to solve by himself.

As the films and television shows make clear, the traveler on the motorcycle was looking for himself within an increasingly industrialized and homogenized society. Although the motorcycle is occasionally demonized, it is overwhelmingly represented as the vehicle for romance with a youthful yearning for freedom.

The diversity of genres that signify this quest for independence is immense. From action thrillers that pit good against evil to apocalyptic visions of world disaster, the motorcycle is repeatedly identified as a protagonist of change. It is cast as both a destructive force and a symbol of redemption, all the while inscribed with sexual overtones. The following timeline and sidebars describe in broad terms the key moments of motorcycle character development in the history of film and television.

The motorcycle is portrayed as the ultimate agent of freedom and risk-taking as Steve McQueen makes his heroic getaway in *The Great Escape.*

1924
Sherlock Jr.
BUSTER KEATON

Buster Keaton creates a hilarious and ironic image of the perils of the 1920s "machine age" as he rides on the handlebars of a motorcycle that has no driver.

1933
Duck Soup
LEO MCCAREY

The motorcycle and sidecar contribute to Fredonia's anarchy in this Marx Brothers' classic, leaving President Rufus T. Firefly at the side of the road.

1949
Orpheus
JEAN COCTEAU

In Cocteau's version of the Greek myth, Death arrives for The Poet in the form of twin leather-clad motorcyclists.

I Was a Male War Bride
HOWARD HAWKS

Cary Grant rides across occupied Germany in a motorcycle sidecar with Ann Sheridan at the controls.

1954
The Wild One
LAZLO BENEDEK

The film that created the movie motorcycling icon. Marlon Brando leads the Black Rebels Club into town looking for a jukebox, kicks, and a little action.

La Strada
FEDERICO FELLINI

A circus strong man drags his assistant/wife across the post-war Italian landscape in a battered three-wheeler.

1957
Motorcycle Gang
EDWARD CAHN

Bad motorcyclists ruin things for the good motorcyclists' club.

1958
Dragstrip Riot
DAVID BRADLEY

Teenage delinquent hot-rodders duke it out with teenage motorcycle gang.

1962
Lawrence of Arabia
DAVID LEAN

Seen from the doomed hero's point of view, T. E. Lawrence's motorcycle ride into oblivion makes for a stunning opening sequence.

Roaring Comedies

Bye Bye Birdie (1963)

Shampoo (1975)

Raising Arizona (1987)

Bikes in Action

Cycle Psycho (1972)

The Mechanic (1972)

Never Say Never Again (1983)

The Killer (1989)

Lethal Weapon 3 (1992)

Rumble in the Bronx (1996)

1963

The Great Escape

JOHN STURGES

Steve McQueen performs in what is perhaps Hollywood's greatest motorcycle scene, fleeing the Nazis by jumping his bike over barbed wire fences.

Scorpio Rising

KENNETH ANGER

Anger's underground classic, a collage of icons of motorcycling and homosexual imagery.

The Leather Boys

SIDNEY J. FURIE

Controversial in its time, a study of British rocker subculture with a homosexual subtext.

1963–65

Beach Party *(1963)*

Bikini Beach *(1964)*

Beach Blanket Bingo *(1965)*

How to Stuff a Wild Bikini *(1965)*

WILLIAM ASHER

From American International's wildly popular "clean teen" series of surfing, dancing, and bathing suits directed by William Asher. Each features Harvey Lembeck as Eric Von Zipper, the moronic leader of a parody of a motorcycle gang based on *The Wild One.*

1964

Roustabout

JOHN RICH

Elvis Presley as a singing drifter touring on his motorcycle. Dressed in leather, Elvis performs "I Got Wheels on My Heels" while astride his red Honda.

1964

Twilight Zone

CAYUGA PRODUCTIONS IN ASSOCIATION WITH CBS TV

Episode "The Black Leather Jackets." Neighbors fear the leather-clad motorcyclists who move in on the block, then discover the worst: the bikers are really aliens intent on contaminating the earth's water supplies.

1966

The Wild Angels

ROGER CORMAN

The biker's philosophy: "We want to be free to ride our machines and not be hassled by The Man." Wildly successful film based on media hype about the Hells Angels, inaugurates a seven-year cycle of biker flicks.

The many films chasing the success of *The Wild Angels* took maximum advantage of the collapse of legal and institutional censorship that held sway during the 1950s. As exploitation films, these productions exploit the new freedoms with obsessive images of nudity, drug use, and explicit violence.

Mods and Rockers

The Wild Guitar (1962)

Crazy Baby (1968)

Quadrophenia (1979)

Streets of Fire (1984)

On the Road

1968

She-Devil on Wheels
HERSCHELL GORDON LEWIS

Taking master Lewis gets in on the biker exploitation frenzy, offering up this biker chick feature in which the Maneaters on Motorbikes gang wreak havoc on a small town.

1967–68

Bike Boy
ANDY WARHOL

Warhol's amalgam of young men, desire, and a working-class biker.

1968

Footage of Evel Knievel's jump at Caesar's Palace

In the jump that made him a household name, the daredevil fails to clear the ramp and crashes spectacularly in the land of high-stakes gambling. Knievel would be unconscious for thirty days.

1969

Easy Rider
DENNIS HOPPER

Taking the bike into the consciousness of the larger culture, Billy and Captain America tour the American West on motorized horseback to the sounds of sixties rock. *Easy Rider* promoted the idea of the customized motorcycle, "the chopper," as a kind of folk art.

Ask the person on the street for a title of a motorcycle movie, and *Easy Rider* is the answer you get. The awesome critical and financial success of the film re-ignited the interest in bike flicks. Examples:

1970

C.C. & Company
(aka Chrome Hearts)
SEYMOUR ROBBIE

Joe Namath and Ann-Margret star in this rebel biker story.

1971

Werewolves on Wheels
MICHAEL LEVESQUE

Bikers turn into werewolves when they fall victims of a satanic spell.

1973

Magnum Force
TED POST

From Clint Eastwood's "Dirty Harry" series of films. Iconographically connects mirrored sunglasses, stormtrooper boots, motorcycles, and rogue police vigilantes.

Electra Glide in Blue
JAMES GUERCIO

The life of a motorcycle cop who rides along Monument Valley–a brutal homicide detective on one side of him and murderous Hippies on the other.

Freewheeling Women

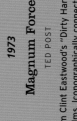

Thrills and Spills

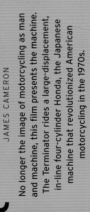

1975
Roller Ball
NORMAN JEWISON

In this violent futuristic tale, the motorcycle becomes a fatal weapon in neo-Roman gladiator games.

Rocky Horror Picture Show
JIM SHARMAN

Amid glam decadence, rocker Meatloaf roars off on a classic cycle.

1976
Kings of the Road—In the Course of Time
WIM WENDERS

A writer and a film projectionist journey together in this sparse black-and-white road movie.

1977–1983
CHiPs
MGM-TV

Across 138 episodes, this light crime drama created a vision of life in the late twentieth century entirely bounded by freeway guardrails.

1979
Mad Max
GEORGE MILLER

In this punk post-apocalypse fantasy, the motorcycle is seen as the representative raw metal machine of human spirit, stripped of the accoutrements of civilization.

1983
The Loveless
KATHRYN BIGELOW

This 1950s period piece speaks to the impulse toward retro that figured the otherwise high-rolling 1980s.

1984
The Terminator
JAMES CAMERON

No longer the image of motorcycling as man and machine, this film presents the machine. The Terminator rides a large-displacement, in-line four-cylinder Honda, the Japanese machine that revolutionized American motorcycling in the 1970s.

Purple Rain
ALBERT MAGNOLI

In this semi-autobiographical debut, the artist formerly known as Prince cruises around on his stylized accessory of a bike.

1985
Pee Wee's Big Adventure
TIM BURTON

In an epic quest for his beloved bicycle, Pee Wee runs into trouble with biker big boys.

Doom and Vroom

Deathsport (1978)

The Road Warrior (1981)

City Limits (1985)

The Running Man (1987)

Terminator 2—Judgment Day (1991)

The Rapture (1991)

1986

Eat the Peach

PETER ORMROD

Inspired by Elvis in *Roustabout*, two out-of-work lads decide to try their luck at motorcycling in this quirky Irish comedy.

1989

Black Rain

RIDLEY SCOTT

New York homicide detective races his Harley on city streets to relax.

1990

Cry-Baby

JOHN WATERS

Waters' nostalgia for the classic 1950s middle-class across-the-tracks romance has Johnny Depp weeping for his wrecked Harley.

1991

Harley Davidson and the Marlboro Man

SIMON WINCER

Bank robbers on bikes run into trouble with the Mob.

1992–93

Renegade

STEPHEN J. CONNELL PRODUCTIONS

Popular crime series in which a framed cop tours the country on a chopper-style Harley, working as a bounty hunter and trying to clear his name.

1993

Sleazy Rider

JOHN MORITSUGU

Underground homage to *Easy Rider* about two girl bikers with bad attitudes who wind up on the wrong end of evil Cruella's shotgun.

1990–94

Roseanne

CARSY-WERNER PRODUCTIONS

Episode **"Born to be Wild."** Title characters resurrect their old Harley from the garage and re-experience moments of their early romance.

1994

She Lives to Ride

ALICE STONE

Stone's documentary profiles five diverse women who have devoted their lives to motorcycling as a business and sport.

1996

Barb Wire

DAVID HOGAN

Based on a comic book character, Pamela Lee Anderson is a "Don't Call Me Babe!" tough chick.

1997

Tomorrow Never Dies

ROGER SPOTTISWOOD

"Never say never again"—that is until Bond reappears in another thrilling motorcycle stunt. In this latest Bond flik he teams up with Hong Kong action superstar Michelle Yeoh.

Cyberbikes

Tron (1982)

Cyclone (1987)

Akira (1988)

Compiled with assistance from

Frank Arnold,

Art Simon, and

Maria-Christina Villaseñor

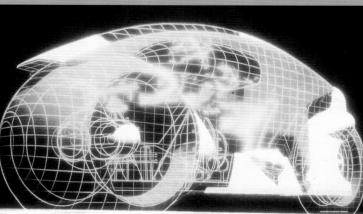

Cinema Vespa *Roman Holiday (1953), Rome Adventure (1962), Jessica (1962), In the French Style (1963)*

Italian Raffaele Alberti astride his Moto Guzzi sets a world record for solo motorcycling on the Saxon-Charrat road, Switzerland, 1948.

The motorcycle

and its cultural influence cover a broad landscape of

contrasting values, personalities, and lifestyles.

From recklessness to absolute control, rebelliousness to social conformity,
the different messages conveyed by the motorcycle and the people who ride them
reflect the diversity and depth of its constituency.

The themes explored through image and narrative in the following four sections attempt to capture
some of the more salient conceptions of the motorcycle in the popular imagination.

The Motorcycle as Icon by Matthew Drutt

Speed and Danger

The motorcycle embodies the ultimate high for thrill-seekers and speed demons. What could be more dangerous than climbing on top of an exposed gasoline-combustion engine and cutting through the air virtually unprotected on a machine that balances on two wheels?

Organized sport racing began as soon as motorcycles became fast enough to consider worth racing. The quest for speed, and victory, is the raison d'être of the professional racer. Zooming around a track at speeds close to 185 mph, one knee skimming above the ground as he rounds a turn, is all in a day's work for him.

As Hunter S. Thompson wrote, "The final measure of any rider's skill is the inverse ratio of his preferred traveling speed to the number of bad scars on his body. It is that simple: If you ride fast and crash, you are a bad rider. If you go slow and crash, you are a bad rider. And if you are a bad rider, you should not ride motorcycles."

It is a sensibility echoed throughout the racing world, and indeed the bike world at large. But danger is ever-present, if masked by the rider's intense desire to achieve the full potential of his machine. Perhaps only the distance of time and the experience of age can bring a different perspective. Retired champion racer Don Emde recently observed, "When we raced professionally it was about winning, not danger. We were more concerned with getting the best sponsors and the right equipment and we didn't focus on getting hurt. People who race professionally are unrealistic about the danger that awaits them. It has something to do with denial. Sure I lost plenty of friends in the business who died in horrible wrecks on the tracks, but I only ever busted up a few bones and never thought much about it. I used to stand on bridges or high places and get the urge to jump just for the thrill of it. That's what racing was like."

The Fastest Men on Two Wheels

Almost too fast for the photographer, German Ernst Henne is captured on film during an attempt at the world record in Wiener Neustadt, 1931.

The Flying Mile

Land speed records are calculated to the thousandth of a second and reflect the time it takes for the rider to cover one mile (or one kilometer). Sometimes called a flying start or the flying mile, the riders are allowed to achieve the maximum speed before they are clocked. There is no limit to the length of the distance covered before timing begins. At the Bonneville Salt Flats in Utah, the run-up is generally four or five miles, depending on the condition of the flats. Flying miles require two runs to be made in opposite directions, one hour apart. The two times are then averaged. Dave Campos set his 1990 record within new parameters, which call for a two-hour interval between runs. His record has not yet been beaten.   —DON VESCO

Skidding on his knees to the finish line, Australian Michael Doohan places first at the 1997 Grand Prix de France, in the 500 km race.

World Records

The first official world record for land speed was secured on April 14, 1920, at Daytona by American Ernie Walker atop a 994cc Indian V-twin (104.12 mph/167.67 km/h). The 1930s saw a raging international battle for the record, with German Ernst Henne and his BMW appearing several times at the top of the heap. American Wilhelm Hertz put an end to a lull in the 1940s with his 1951 record of 180 mph/338.092 km/h riding an NSU 499 near Ingolstadt, Germany. Recently, American Don Vesco was clocked at 318.598 mph/509.757 km/h on his 2030cc Kawasaki at Bonneville in 1978. The latest record within the newly revised parameters belongs to another American, Dave Campos, whose record of 322.149 mph/518.66 km/h was set at Albuquerque on a 3000cc Harley-Davidson in 1990.   —DON VESCO

In 1950 Roland R. Free—atop his British-Vincent motorcycle in prone position to cut down wind resistance—established a new American speed record of 1 mile at 156.71 mph at Bonneville Salt Flats, Utah.

Stunts

The spectacle of impending danger and gravity-defying feats displayed in sport racing is even more thrilling in professional stunts. Like racers, too, stunt drivers focus proudly on their craft; at the same time, they court danger deliberately.

Bud Ekins, who performed stunts for Steve McQueen in *Bullitt* as well as in numerous films and television programs, has noted that "anybody that gets hurt doing motorcycle stunts is stupid. It's got to be super-planned, not hurried. But I guess I'm stupid 'cause I got hurt plenty of times. I once did a stunt for Charlton Heston in *Omega Man* and had this Black girl hanging on the back of the bike with me. I could tell she was nervous because of how tight she was holding on to me. She asked me 'Are you scared?' and I said 'Hell no, I'm not scared!' and she said, 'Then why is your heart beating so fast?' Well, I thought, it does get your adrenaline going when you fly through the air at 70 mph without a helmet on."

Stunt performer Ken Mackow has been even more unabashed about his approach: "My first big jump was on July 3, 1974. I cleared 16 cars at Ascot Park in Gardena, California. In clearing the 80-foot gap, I broke Evel Knievel's track record of 15 cars. On July 17, 1974, I returned to Ascot Park to try and break my track record of 16 cars and also break Evel Knievel's record jump of 19 cars. Instead, I was seven mph too slow, landed short and broke my body instead. I hit the end of the landing ramp. I was thrown over 100 feet. I broke my back, left leg, both thumbs, and my jaw. I was laid up for eight weeks. On July 20, 1975, I set another world record when I rode my motorcycle through a 157-foot, seven-inch-long Tunnel of Fire. This record was listed in the paperback edition of the 1976 *Guinness Book of World Records*. In 1977, the Tunnel of Fire category was dropped from the record book because another daredevil attempted to break my record and was killed in the process. Guinness said that any tunnel longer than mine would be suicide and they did not want to be responsible for another dead daredevil."

(top, left) A daredevil motorcyclist gears up for his jump over three surprisingly calm people.
(top, right) Eddie Kidd clears a lineup of cars in an amazing jump of 1982. (right) Captain M. R. Potter performs a spectacular fire jump as part of the Royal Signals Display at Catterick Camp, Yorkshire.

Protection on wheels: a "dress rehearsal" by a British police motorcycle escort, riding in perfect "V" formation, for President Eisenhower's arrival in London.

John (Larry Wilcox) and Ponch (Erik Estrada), costars of television's bike cop drama *CHiPs*,
are the quintessential squeaky-clean highway patrol officers.

Law *and Order*

Motorcycles are, in many ways, at odds with law enforcement. Loud and fast, they disrupt the peace and quiet of domestic communities when they come screaming down a street at full throttle and break all kinds of laws as they whine down a highway at speeds of over 100 mph.

The intensity of reaction can be noted in comments such as one writer's belief expressed in *The New York Times* in 1997: "The police should view motorcycle noise as a criminal assault." But the law has also claimed motorcycles as their own, fighting fire with fire, as it were, with motorcycle divisions comprising their elite corps. The by-the-book image of the motorcycle cop, venerated in the television program *CHiPS*, is the modern-day version of Tom Mix or Roy Rogers; the lone sheriff on his trusty steed ferreting out bad guys with a tip of his hat is today the austere, mirror-shaded county cop lying in wait behind a billboard:

"You in a heap 'o trouble, boooy!"

"I THINK LEGISLATIVE ASSAULTS ON MOTORCYCLISTS ARE TOTALLY EMOTIONAL, DISPROPORTIONATE AND TOTALLY UNFAIR. . . . THEY ARE INSTIGATED AND IMPLEMENTED BY PEOPLE WHO KNOW NOTHING ABOUT MOTORCYCLING, BUT HAVE A PREJUDICE. . . . IT'S EASY TO CURB THE FREEDOMS OF OTHERS WHEN YOU SEE NO IMMEDIATE IMPACT ON YOUR OWN."

Malcolm Forbes

(left) No helmet in sight—an arrest is made. (center) A bike cop tries his hand at community service with a group of free spirits. (right) Police insignia emblazoned on a Harley-Davidson highway patrol motorcycle.

Confronting the laws that undercut a motorcyclist's "freedom of expression," or perhaps "freedom of experience"—fundamentally the right to ride the machine and the right not to wear a helmet—have helped unify bikers, giving them causes célèbres to which they respond, often quite formally. ABATE (A Brotherhood Against Totalitarian Enactments) is at the forefront of responses to the laws most universally reviled by motorcyclists—helmet laws.
Its research notes:

Rider Training vs. Helmet Laws
The accident totals and the fatality totals have shown a steady decrease as rider training increases, with no discernible change at the inception of the mandatory adult helmet law.

Helmet Laws Not Proven Effective
Since 1983, the fatality rate for motorcyclists has fluctuated between two and three per 100 accidents, with and without mandated helmet usage.

Highest Risk Riders Still Under Requirement
Endorsed riders 20 years old and younger are 18 times more likely to be involved in some sort of collision.

Facts Do NOT Support Public Burden Theory
Motorcyclists are just as likely to be insured as other road trauma victims, and their injuries typically cost less to fix.

Hardcore Harley riders say, "Live to ride, ride to live," and leave your lid at home.

(right) "The Rules of the Road," from *The Motor Cycle Book for Boys*, 1928.

(far right) Police motorcyclist brigade leads a funeral procession for a slain state trooper, 1995.

Fundamentally it is the biker's freedom of expression that is at issue. The New York State Vehicle Law, for example, which states that "no person shall operate on a public highway a motorcycle on which the handlebars or grips are more than fifteen inches higher than the seat or saddle for the operator," is another source of controversy for bikers who want to customize their machines and are curbed by what they deem to be an arbitrary limitation.

Another area of legal intervention is in rules of behavior for motorcycling's time-honored convoy "runs." From Hells Angels gangs to presidential motorcades, group riding unifies bikers as well as requiring conformity to a group hierarchy in a quasi-militaristic fashion (including "officers" of the club, the use of "colors," and an "out-on-patrol" sensibility). The Blue Knights MC (International Brotherhood of Law Enforcement Officers) has "rules of the road" for informal rides that stress common sense, of course, but even more emphasize biker unity and group order. For example:

Do not fool around (horse play) when riding with the group.
Any member observing another member fooling around when in formation should discuss it with that member and attempt to clear up the situation. If it should persist, bring it to the attention of the Road Captain or one of his Assistants.

While on any run, the Road Captain or his assistant will ride in front.
The President may ride alongside or just behind the Captain depending on the formation in use. In the absence of the Road Captain and the assistants, whomever the Captain appoints will ride point.

Line up for a ride as follows.
Road Captain, President, full color wearing members, followed by the Sgt. at Arms, then by prospective members, non-members and bringing up the rear the assistant Road Captains and the Tail Gunner. Once you are in position keep it for the remainder of the ride.

Anticipate your next move and those of the group.
With regard to remaining alert, as one of a group, you must remember that the Road Captain from time to time will be giving a hand signal to execute a maneuver (pass slow-moving vehicle, make a turn, etc.) He will be taking into consideration the size of the group and the distance necessary to get the club from one lane to another safely. Each members assistance in executing the maneuver safely and smoothly will be of great assistance. The rear Road Captain(s) will help the group by getting out into the lane following the forward Captain's signal. By doing this he will help secure the chance to execute the maneuver freely and safely. Stay in position during any lane change or direction maneuver.

"I am going to Stop."   "I am about to turn to the Right."

"I am about to turn to the Left."   "I am slowing down!"

Hand signals are necessary to formation riding and integral to motorcycling overall. They are used for safety and they help
to create a good club image. Below are listed the standard hand signals as adopted by the Blue Knights MC:

Stop: Left hand extended downward and palm facing backward. **Right Turn:** Left arm upright and hand extended. **Left Turn:** Left arm extended straight out and hand extended. **A Turnaround Signal:** This is used for group riding as well as signaling an individual rider approaching. **Single File Riding:** Arm extended over head with index finger pointed up means single file riding, used for narrow, winding roads, road obstructions and hazards. **Close Up Formation:** Left arm moved in an up-and-down motion (pumping) with fist closed. This action means tighten up or close riding formation, catch up and stay close. The Road Captain will use this signal to execute a group maneuver. **Road Hazard:** Pointing downward is to warn fellow riders of pot holes and debris in the road. **Staggered Riding:** Hand straight up with four fingers extended waving side to side. Staggered riding is used on open roads and where there are a lot of turns. This style allows the rider some leeway for drifting. **V Signal:** Two fingers indicate dual riding style or two abreast where permitted. **Other Hand Signals:** Pointing to your gas tank means you have switched to your reserve. Blow horn to alert Captain. Waving the hand back and forth with arm extended to the side means come up to me or pass me.

A chopper trike on a country road, Colorado, 1971.

Outlaw and *Rebellion*

The renegade biker is the most popular stereotype of motorcycle subculture celebrated in film, television, music, and the popular imagination. Clad in leather and projecting an image of willful defiance of all socially acceptable codes of behavior, the outlaw biker represents the final frontier of rebellion. The outlaw represents anti-establishment sentiment—particularly with regard to helmet laws—but also patriotic pride in the USA's freedom of individual expression (the Harley—as opposed to the imported bike—is part and parcel of this patriotic symbolism). As a banner for the infamous annual biker rally in Sturgis, South Dakota, reads, "Send flag burners to Sturgis. We explain things better than the Supreme Court."

The outlaw biker's identity is prized, not only in distinction to those outside the biker community but also to those bikers who do not subscribe to the loose code of outlaw values. This debate is constantly alive. As the *Angry Biker* homepage on the Internet notes, "What is the 'True American Biker?' It may be easier to say who is not a biker—like RUBs and yuppie scum, but that would be too simple. *Angry Biker* represents the free-spirited element of the biking community that stands up for his rights, and does not take orders from others on how to think. True Bikers think for themselves, and answer to the American ideals of fair play and the rights guaranteed to us by the Constitution of the United States. Patriotic, yes, but not necessarily flag wavers. Outlaws? Perhaps, but no more than our elected officials."

Captain America (Peter Fonda): "NO, I MEAN IT, YOU'VE GOT A NICE PLACE HERE.
IT'S NOT EVERY MAN WHO CAN LIVE OFF THE LAND. YOU DO YOUR OWN THING IN YOUR OWN TIME. YOU SHOULD BE PROUD."
George Hanson (Jack Nicholson): "I MEAN IT IS REAL HARD TO BE FREE WHEN YOU ARE BOUGHT AND SOLD IN THE MARKETPLACE."

Easy Rider (1969)

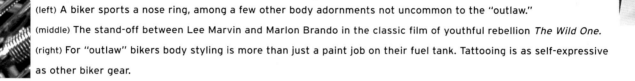

(left) A biker sports a nose ring, among a few other body adornments not uncommon to the "outlaw."

(middle) The stand-off between Lee Marvin and Marlon Brando in the classic film of youthful rebellion *The Wild One*.

(right) For "outlaw" bikers body styling is more than just a paint job on their fuel tank. Tattooing is as self-expressive as other biker gear.

And as one Internet debater has written:

Nothwithstanding the beating the biker image has taken in films and media reporting, bikers have somewhat enjoyed the notoriety the "bad" image gave them, as it kept out the squares and formed a brotherhood of social outcasts that enjoyed a semi-exclusive culture. The Honda motorcycle commercials of the '60s proclaiming that "you meet the nicest people on a Honda" helped to create the diversion (sic.) between Jap motorcycle riders and the hardcore (mainly) Harley riders, which also helped fuel the "biker" image. Starting right around 1984–85, "Hollywood Bikers" appeared on the scene and all of sudden owning a Harley was the yuppie thing, just like BMW cars. The newbie yuppie wanna-bes that have bought into the "biker" scene are now busy trying to clean up everybody's image, but as far as we are concerned we rather liked the old image. "Biker trash" you say? Yuppie scum is more like it.

But there are plenty of retorts:

Since when does anybody have the freaking right to judge a fellow motorcycle rider. . . . Why don't you start minding your own business and worry less about the other guy? . . . Motorcycling is about having the big thumping iron just between your legs and enjoy the scenery together with getting from A to B.

Choppers, with their high 'n' wide handlebars, and the open road—what more could one need?

(left) A bird's eye view of one of the sexiest bikes around—the Ducati 916. A phenomenon, the Ducati is more than an enthusiasm—it is a passion.

Pamela Anderson Lee stars in the lead role as a leather-clad vixen in the 1996 David Hogan film *Barb Wire*.

Mystique and Sexuality

Motorcycles are surrounded by an aura of sexual power and mystique unparalleled by any other mode of transportation.

The raw design of early bikes suggests the rough rider brave enough to straddle an exposed engine and ride at high speeds without safety gear. More modern bikes are endowed with the sleek elegance of high fashion and design, with every rivet, gasket, and exhaust pipe suggestive of taste and refinement. These two opposite ends of the spectrum, and the vast range of attitudes bracketed within them, continue to be perpetuated both by the design and marketing of new machines as well as by the popular impressions conveyed through film, television, and advertising.

RIDING WOMEN ON THE HOT MACHINES.
SAY THE BEST THINGS THEY EVER SEEN.
BIG V-TWIN, HONEY BACK IT ON IN.
LET ME FEEL IT RUNNING UP AND DOWN MY SKIN. . .
THEN REV IT UP AGAIN!!!

Patty-Greer Roche, "Roaring Thunder"

The Mystique of the Ducati by David M. Gross

There are few things that make you feel sexy, so free, so adventuresome, so full of life as a shiny red Ducati 916 full of fuel. No wonder bad-boy Brit bike magazines like to run photo spreads with boys in bed nude with their 916s or Monsters. Rounding the turn on a moutain pass in the San Padre moutains on a 916 lets you dream of Superbike World Championships and great Ducati riders like Troy Corser and Carl Fogarty.

A Ducati conveys the sensuality, the texture, the eroticism of the Italian motoring tradition like nothing else. Ducati motorcycles are not volume-produced by a giant industrial conglomerate. They are not designed by committee. And they do not come in dozens of sizes, shapes, and colors. The Ducati is that rare object —a functional sports machine that is also a work of art.

Times have changed for women riders: (left) A woman in the wind. (middle) Most biker gear for women is barely distinguishable from that for men. (right) Taking a break from racing.

Despite the motorcycle's history as a vehicle dominated by male sport and recreation, today's biker is as likely to be a woman as a man. No longer relegated to sitting behind a driver or gracing the bike as a sex object, women now ride alone or band together in groups and enjoy the passion and exhilaration of riding that was previously reserved for men.

Consider some comments from online magazines and Websites:

I am not some radical who thinks wearing a bandanna is more macho than wearing a helmet. I have four children, I'm a grandmother, and I am a legal assistant and have worked for the same firm for 24 years. I own a mobile home park and 13 rental properties, and am probably one of the most conservative people you will ever meet. My form of recreation and stress relief just happens to be riding my Harley up to Oakwood Lake to watch the ducks. HARLEY MOM, *HARLEY MOM'S WEBSITE.*

I ride as if all the cages are out to get me and so far, I've managed to miss the ones that actually were. . . . Like everyone else I ride for the freedom.
ALICE MACPHERSON, *WOMEN OF THE ROAD.*

Recently I was over a friend's house for lunch, came out to get on my bike, and about made a guy gardening nearby drop his teeth; "Nice bike," sez he. "Thanks," sez I. Silence while I get the bike ready to roll. Then he clears his throat and sez, "You know, I never expected to see a young lady come out to that bike." Hah! I love busting up people's stereotypes. LEIGH ANN, BERKELEY, CALIFORNIA, *WOMEN OF THE ROAD.*

My First Bike

Owning your first motorcycle is a rite of passage possibly even more symbolic than your first car, signifying a heightened sense of personal freedom and release. The memory of that first bike is that of a first romance.

My first motorcycle was a 1948 Harley 74. The year was 1967, and my contemporaries were all trying to talk their parents into buying them Honda 90s or Yamaha 200s. The Harley was big, crude, and well-used—it belched balls of fire out of the air cleaner when I tried to kick-start it, and did the same from the exhaust pipes going down hills. It spit oil all over my boots, woke my neighbors, shook, shuddered, and pounded with life. But for all its faults, it was, to me, the best material possession the world had to offer. It represented escape, mobility, power, freedom, and excitement—that Harley let me breathe and see beyond the confusion of the times. DENNIS STEMP, CREATIVE DIRECTOR, *IRONWORKS* MAGAZINE

The first bike I owned was a Yamaha RS100, a single-cylinder commuter. I remember my dad teaching me clutch control outside the shop. The terrifying acceleration and vibration and the almost irresistible wind blast at a teeth-gritting 55 mph made me feel as though I'd get blown off the back. The bike did 20,000 miles in a year and never went wrong. RUPERT PAUL, EDITOR-IN-CHIEF, *MODERN MOTORCYCLING*

My parents made me promise as a teenager that I would never ride a motorcycle, but at the age of sixteen I was secretly riding my first bike, a Harley Panhead 1956 chopper. At the age of twenty-two I was hit by a car, resulting in many broken bones. I vowed never to get on a bike again. However, I couldn't shake my love for motorcycles. In fact, it led me to find an occupation where I could be paid to ride a motorcycle. A major responsibility of our job is escorting visiting dignitaries and U.S. government officials with motorcycle convoys. RAY SMITH, DEPUTY SHERIFF, MIAMI/DADE COUNTY

I got my first bike in college: a Honda, just 175cc. It had no registration or insurance, temperamental brakes, and an even more fickle first gear. When my then-boyfriend came out to visit he got hooked on riding, too, and since we both make particularly bad pillion partners we now both have motorcycles. We traded up for Harley-Davidsons and rode to New Orleans for the honeymoon. ALESSANDRA BOCCO, EDITOR, HENRY HOLT & COMPANY

Over fifty years ago, my father bought me, begrudgingly, my first and only bike—a 1921 single-cylinder Cleveland—from a secondhand dealer for twenty-five dollars. My mother's best friend told her that they were deathtraps. The clutch was bad and the body was in tough shape. But it was good transportation for a college student. It has sat around for years. Somehow, I never wanted to sell it. I like mechanical things. CHARLES W. PACHNER, CHAIRMAN EMERITUS, FRENKEL & CO., INC.

126

When I was fourteen, I walked past our local Indian dealership every day on my way to school. My dad's enthusiasm for his own 1916 Indian Powerplus had rubbed off on me. I fell in love with a 1929 Indian Scout the dealer had for seventy dollars. I was so paranoid that someone would buy the Scout before I could afford to purchase it, so I went in the shop every day to check. Once I had the money, the dealer informed me that my dad would have to sign the bill of sale, as I was too young. GEORGE YAROCKI, G. L. YAROCKI COMPANY (SPECIALIZING IN ANTIQUE MOTORCYCLE LITERATURE)

Acknowledgments

This publication was a team effort, with a variety of individuals contributing their talent, expertise, assistance, and encouragement. In particular, I would like to thank all of the authors for their contributions to the various parts of the book. Vanessa Rocco, curatorial assistant at the Guggenheim Museum, was a phenomenal asset to the project, assisting with and contributing to every aspect of the book. Sandy Gilbert and Charles Miers at Universe Publishing were generous with both their ideas and their patience, and made significant contributions to the shape of the publication along the way. Sandy was particularly instrumental in helping to locate many of the images and contributors, and was a vital liaison between the Museum and the designer. Chuck Routhier did more than devise a handsome design for the book; he assisted with the editorial process and was central to its success at nearly every level. He was assisted in the design by Fred Schaub. I am most indebted to Anthony Calnek, Director of Publications at the Guggenheim Museum, for his support and encouragement throughout the project. I would also like to thank him for first suggesting my involvement.

For their assistance with research and visual materials, I would like to thank the following: Ilaria Fusina (Universe Publishing); Glenn Bator (Otis Chandler Vintage Museum of Transportation and Wildlife); Jeff Ray and Brian Slark (The Barber Vintage Motorsports Museum); Daniel Statnekov; Kevin Cameron; Erbo Hermanns, David Robb, Jutta Quade, Suzanne Conrad, and Lou Rodriguez (BMW AG); Garry Stuart; Stuart Munger; Bruce Fairey and David Gross (Ducati Motor SpA); Gary Christopher (Honda); Conrad Bodman (Barbican Art Center); Dave Hansen (Langlitz Leathers); Fred Wyse (Vanson Leathers); Marc Rona (American Dream Machine); Larry Spielfogel; the editors of *Cycle World*; Aaron Fitch (American Motorcyclist Association); Randy Leffingwell; Don Vesco; George Yarocki; Bob Cox (The Cox Group, Inc.); David Leddick; Bud Ekins; Don Emde; Joanne Morelli (Screen Actor's Guild); Marc and Aaron Freidus; Professor Charles Falco (University of Arizona, Tucson); Buzz Kanter (*American Iron*); Fred Eaton (Old Britts Motorcycle Shop); and Dennis Scully (Petersen Publishing Company).

Claudia Schmuckli, curatorial assistant at the Guggenheim Museum, assisted with translations of selected texts, and Sarah Botts provided invaluable assistance at the beginning stages of the book. The editing of the book was also a team effort, and I am most grateful to Domenick Ammirati (Guggenheim Museum); Bonnie Eldon and David McAninch (Universe Publishing); Alessandra Bocco; and Kerry Acker. Finally, my thanks to Elizabeth White and Robin Key at Rizzoli for aiding in the production of the book.

Photography Credits

Keep the rubber side down and the shiny side up. . . .